Essential
Laptops

Kevin Wilson

Elluminet Press

www.elluminetpress.com

Essential Laptops

Publisher: Elluminet Press
Director: Kevin Wilson
Lead Editor: Steven Ashmore
Technical Reviewer: Mike Taylor, Robert Ashcroft
Copy Editors: Joanne Taylor, James Marsh
Proof Reader: Robert Ashcroft
Indexer: James Marsh
Cover Designer: Kevin Wilson

eBook versions and licenses are also available for most titles. Any source code or other supplementary materials referenced by the author in this text is available to readers at

www.elluminetpress.com/resources

For detailed information about how to locate your book's source code, go to

www.elluminetpress.com/resources

Table of Contents

About the Author

Kevin Wilson has made a career out of technology and showing others how to use it. After earning a master's degree in computer science, software engineering, and multimedia systems, Kevin worked as a tutor and college instructor, helping students master such subjects as multimedia, computer literacy and information technology. He currently serves as Elluminet Press Publishing's senior writer and director, he periodically teaches computing at college in South Africa and serves as an IT trainer in England. His books have become a valuable resource among the students in England, South Africa and our partners in the United States.

Kevin's motto is clear: "If you can't explain something simply, you haven't understood it well enough." To that end, he has created the Computer Essentials series, in which he breaks down complex technological subjects into smaller, easy-to-follow steps that students and ordinary computer users can put into practice.

Acknowledgements

Thanks to all the staff at Luminescent Media & Elluminet Press for their passion, dedication and hard work in the preparation and production of this book.

To all my friends and family for their continued support and encouragement in all my writing projects.

To all my colleagues, students and testers who took the time to test procedures and offer feedback on the book

Finally thanks to you the reader for choosing this book. I hope it helps you to use your computer with greater ease.

Chapter 1

Choosing a Laptop

Choosing a laptop can often be confusing as there is a lot of promotional and technical words and phrases floating around.

In this section we'll go through the most common information you'll most likely need when shopping for a laptop.

We'll take a look at some common specifications and try to decode all the technical jargon, so you can be confident when shopping.

What are you using it for?

There are thousands of laptops to choose from with just as many different price ranges and specifications to complicate things even more.

The first question to ask yourself is, what are you intending to use your laptop for. What are your needs? How much do you want to spend? £200, £400, £1000 or £2000?

Common Tasks

As you can see from the scale below, the further down the list you go, the more power (RAM, CPU, Video & HDD) you need.

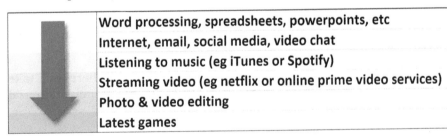

	Word processing, spreadsheets, powerpoints, etc
	Internet, email, social media, video chat
	Listening to music (eg iTunes or Spotify)
	Streaming video (eg netflix or online prime video services)
	Photo & video editing
	Latest games

You should take all these things into consideration when buying your machine. For example, if you are just using your machine to type some documents, check your email and browse the internet, you perhaps don't need the most powerful machine you can find as a lot of that power is expensive and could be wasted.

On the other hand if you do a lot of video editing or photography or play the latest games you would need as much power as you can afford.

Understanding Laptop Specifications

When shopping for a laptop, you'll not doubt come across system specifications such as the one shown below.

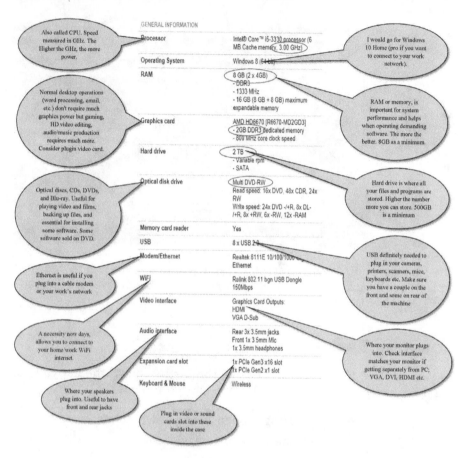

There is a lot of technical jargon in these specifications, here we'll take a moment to go through a commonly found system specification and what each section means.

Lets start at the top: the processor.

What Processor?

The CPU or processor is the brain of the computer and responds to all the commands you give the computer. It is one of the primary factors in determining the power of the system. Measured in Gigahertz, the higher the number, the more powerful the processor.

This is where things get a bit confusing. There are a lot of different processors out there with different numbers and series. However it all boils down to a few numbers to take note of, I've highlighted these in bold. Lets take a look at some common ones.

Intel Pentium / Celeron. These chips are common in cheap laptops, and offer the slowest performance, but can handle tasks such as web browsing, email and document editing. You'd be better off spending a bit extra and going with a Core i3 or i5.

Intel Core i3. Performance is about entry level for basic computer usage such as web browsing, email, social media, word processing, music and looking at a few photos.

AMD A, FX or E Series. Found on low-cost laptops, AMD's processors provide decent performance for the money that's good enough for web browsing, internet, email, streaming films or tv, photos and music, as well as word processing etc. For example:

> AMD **A6**-9220 APU 2.5GHz
> AMD Quad-Core Processor **FX**-9830P

Intel Core i5. If you're looking for a mainstream laptop with the best combination of price and performance, get one with an Intel Core i5 CPU. Always make sure the model number ends with a 'U', HK, or 'HQ' - these offer better performance. For example:

> Intel Core i5-7200**U**
> Intel Core i5-<u>7300**HQ**</u>

Also the higher the number after 'i5', eg 7300, the better the performance.

Intel Core i7. The successor to the Core i5.

AMD Ryzen Series. High powered chips from AMD designed to compete with Intel Core i5 and Core i7. Great alternative to Intel chips and good for gaming and high powered laptops. For example:

> AMD 8-Core **Ryzen R7** 1700

Operating System

As well as all the hardware and peripherals, you need software to make the computer work. The first piece of software that is needed is called an Operating System. This could be Windows 10 on a PC

Mac OS if you're on a Mac laptop.

This Operating System provides you with a user interface where you can use various tools called programs or software to do your work. For example, Microsoft Office is a software application package that allows you to create documents, presentations, spreadsheets and so on. Photoshop is a program for editing photos. This software runs on the Operating System.

Memory (RAM)

The memory or RAM is the computer's workspace. Do not confuse with the Hard Disk Drive (HDD).

If you are typing a document in Microsoft Word, both Microsoft Word and your document are loaded into and stored in the computer's memory (RAM) while you are working on it. When you save your document, it is saved to your Hard Disk. Usually measured in GigaBytes. Eg: 8GB, 16GB etc.

Hard Disk - HDD or SSD?

The hard disk (also called a hard drive) is like a filing cabinet and permanently stores all your documents, photographs, music, your operating system (such as Microsoft Windows) and your installed software (such as Microsoft Word)

When you start up an application such as Microsoft word, the Microsoft word software is loaded up off the hard disk into the computer's memory (or ram), where you can work on your documents. Usually measured in Gigabytes and Terabytes, eg 500GB, 1TB, 4TB.

SSDs perform much like a Hard Disk but are extremely fast and also extremely expensive.

These drives are being used in smaller laptops/notebook computers and on some tablet computers where you don't require large amounts of storage space.

These drives can also be useful where you need fast data transfer rates, such as for video editing, playing games and recording audio/video.

These can be over 2TB, however large capacities are expensive. The average size in use is about 250GB

CD/DVD/Bluray drive

Another dying breed, this drive allows you to play CDs, watch DVDs or Blu-Ray movies that come on a disk. Some of the latest laptops don't include these, however if you need one, you can buy external USB DVD or Blu-Ray drives.

You can also create your own. Most of these drives have a "writer" function that allows you to copy your own data onto a blank disk; this could be your photographs, documents or your home movies.

USB Ports

USB stands for Universal Serial Bus and is a universal connection used to connect all different types of peripherals to your computer as easy as possible using the same connection type.

These ports connect mice, keyboards, scanners, printers, web cams, digital cameras, memory sticks, external hard drives, and so on.

USB 3.0, shown below left, was released on 12 November 2008, with a data rate of around 4 Gbps and is much faster than USB 2.0.

USB 2.0, shown below right, was released in April 2000, with a maximum data rate of 480 Mbps.

USB 3.0 ports are colour coded in blue, while USB 2.0 ports are colour coded in black.

The smaller USB pictured below left is called micro USB and the one next to it is called mini USB.

WiFi

WiFi allows you to connect to a wireless network, also called a Wireless LAN and is usually broadcasting on a frequency of 2.4GHz and 5GHz radio bands. Most WiFi routers broadcast using Wireless G, N or AC, so make sure these are specified in the laptop specification.

Wireless LANs are usually password protected to keep them private and to prevent unwanted visitors using your WiFi. WiFi networks usually have a network name often called an SSID.

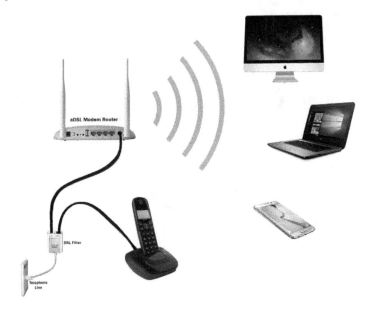

Ethernet

Most of the time you'll connect to the internet using the WiFi on your laptop. Ethernet is used to connect to a network or to your cable modem if you are not using WiFi. These cables look like this.

One end plugs into the Ethernet port on the side of your laptop.

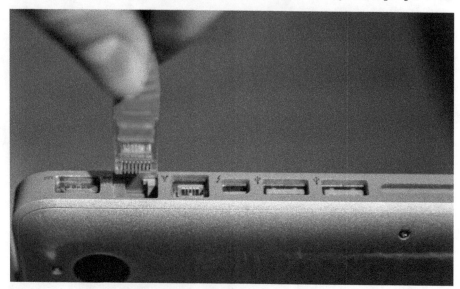

The other end plugs into an Ethernet port on the back of your router.

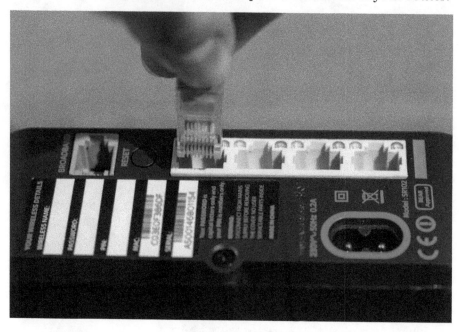

If you are using WiFi to connect to the internet, you don't need to use the Ethernet cable.

Video Interfaces

These interfaces or ports are useful if you want to connect your laptop to a TV or a projector. This is good if you are giving presentations or if you just want to enjoy a movie or TV program. TVs usually connect using HDMI while most projectors will accept all three.

DVI - Digital Video Interface is a video display interface used to connect a video source (eg your computer) to a display device, such as an HD ready TV, computer monitor or projector.

DVI can get a bit confusing, as there are a number of different connectors. Here is a summary.

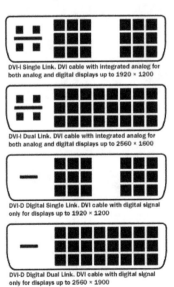

DVI-I Single Link. DVI cable with integrated analog for both analog and digital displays up to 1920 × 1200

DVI-I Dual Link. DVI cable with integrated analog for both analog and digital displays up to 2560 × 1600

DVI-D Digital Single Link. DVI cable with digital signal only for displays up to 1920 × 1200

DVI-D Digital Dual Link. DVI cable with digital signal only for displays up to 2560 × 1900

Chapter 1: Choosing a Laptop

HDMI - High Definition Media Interface, is a combined audio/video interface for carrying video and audio data from a High Definition device such as a games console or computer to a high end computer monitor, video projector, or High Definition digital television.

Pictured below is Standard HDMI & Micro HDMI.

VGA - Video Graphics Array is a 15-pin connector found on many computers and laptops and is used to connect to projectors, computer monitors and LCD television sets.

VGA is quite old technology now days and many of the latest laptops no longer have this port, so it's worth checking if you have a TV or projector that only has VGA ports. Modern TVs and Projectors however will have HDMI ports.

Audio Ports

The 1/8" (3.5mm) Phono Jack, also known as an audio jack, headphone jack or jack plug, is commonly used to connect speakers or headphones to a computer, laptop, tablet or MP3 player and carries analogue audio signals.

The audio port is usually on the side of your laptop. Sometimes there are two ports, one for headphones/speakers and one for a microphone. They are both the same size port so make sure you look for either a headphone symbol or a green port if you're plugging in headphones or speakers.

Graphics Card

The graphics card, sometimes called a graphics adapter or video card is responsible for processing all the graphics, images, video and pretty much anything you see on your screen.

You won't need to worry too much about the graphics card unless you intend on playing the latest games or going to use graphic and photo editing software. In this case you'll need to find the fastest graphics card you can with the most Video RAM.

Screen Size

Laptop screens vary in size and are usually between 13" and 17". A 15" screen is usually the average size.

Remember, you measure the screen size from corner to corner. This particular laptop has a 15.6" screen.

Touch Pad

I personally hate the touch pad that comes as standard on a laptop. I find it infuriating and tiresome to use for any length of time but is useful if you are not using your laptop on a table. I would suggest you get yourself a good wireless mouse.

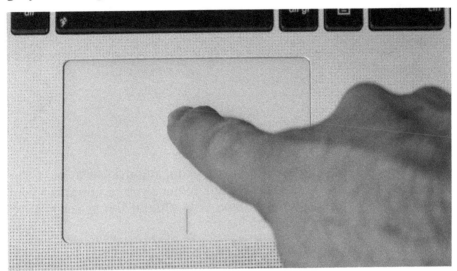

Mouse

A wireless mouse is usually good for using with a laptop. You can get either a bluetooth mouse or wireless mouse.

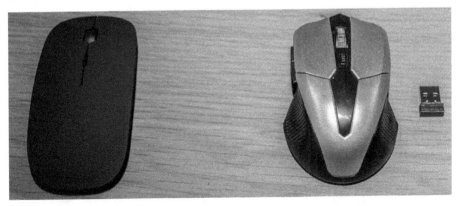

If you go with bluetooth, make sure your laptop has bluetooth capability, otherwise go for a wireless mouse. Wireless mice come with a small dongle you plug into a USB port on the side of your laptop.

Setting up your Laptop

Setting up your laptop is usually straightforward. The first thing you should do once you've unpacked your laptop from its box, is to plug in the power adapter and charge the battery.

Once the battery is installed and charged fully, you can open up the lid and turn on the power.

Windows 10 will normally boot up and take you through some initial setup - this is usually entering your Microsoft Account email and password and your WiFi password.

Setting up your Laptop

The first thing you'll need to do is install the battery. Then once the battery is installed, you can plug in the power adapter. Some laptops have a battery built in and if there is no battery slot on the back then you can skip this step.

Install the Battery

On most laptops, the battery slides in or slots into the back panel of the laptop casing. Not all laptops are the same however.

Make sure the electrical contacts are in line with the contacts on your laptop as shown below.

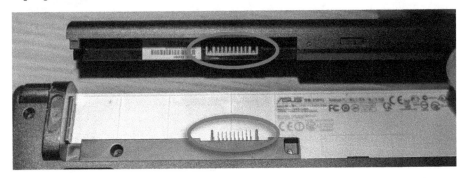

The battery should slide into the slot. You'll hear a light click when the battery is in place.

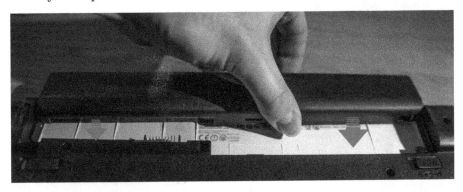

Slide the lock slider to lock the battery in place

Plug In & Power Up

Plug the end of the power adapter into the DC IN port on the side or back of the laptop.

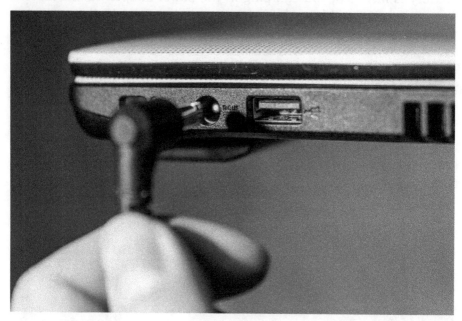

Next plug the mains power cord into the back of the power adapter if required.

Plug the end of the power cord into a spare wall socket and turn on the power.

Laptop Ports

Not all laptops are the same, however they usually have the same ports, it's just that they may be located in a slightly different location. On our laptop we have these ports.

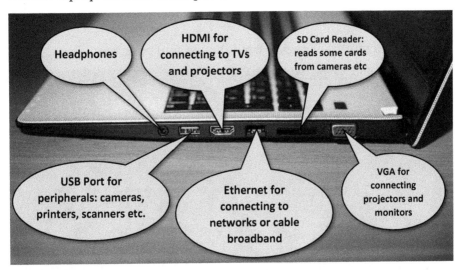

On the other side of your laptop, you might have more ports or a CD/DVD/BluRay disk drive. Not all laptops have this, some don't have any drive at all.

If the drive is present, you can open them by pressing the small eject button on the side, shown above.

Running Windows the First Time

If you've just bought a new laptop with Windows 10, or just installed a fresh copy, you'll need to run through the initial set up procedure.

Regional Settings

Select your country or region from the list and click 'yes'.

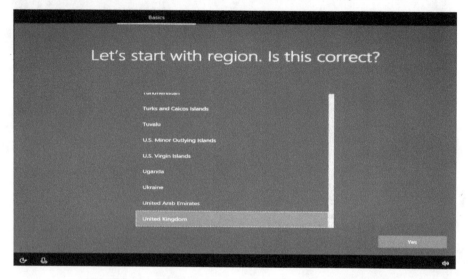

Select keyboard layout for your country, then click 'yes'. Skip secondary keyboard if you don't have one.

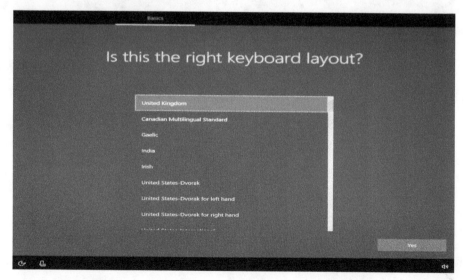

Terms Of Use

On the terms and agreements page click on 'Accept'.

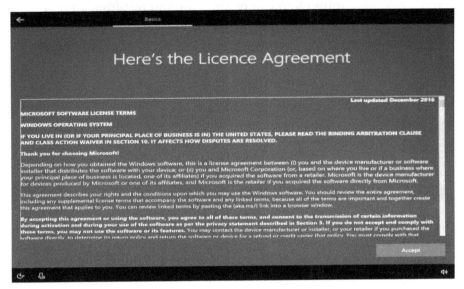

Connect to your WiFi

Select your WiFi network from the list of detected networks. This is usually printed on your router/modem or you can find out from your service provider. Click 'connect' from the box that appears.

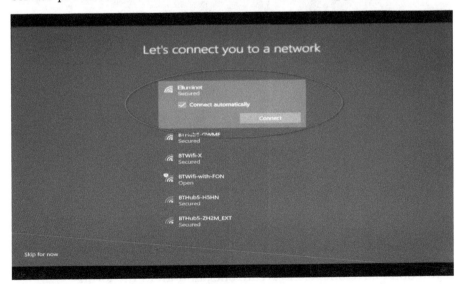

Enter WiFi Password

Enter the password for your WiFi network. This will be printed on the back of your router/modem or you can find out from your service provider.

Click 'yes' to the prompt if you are on your home WiFi network. Click 'no' if you're using a public wifi hotspot such as a library, coffee shop or airport - you don't want other people to see you on a public network.

Sign in for the First Time

Sign in with your Microsoft Account email address and password, then click 'next'. This allows you to make use of OneDrive, email, purchase apps from the App Store, buy music and films.

If you don't have one, click 'create one', and fill in the form.

Set a PIN Code

Click 'Set a PIN code', then tap in your code, if you want the extra security. This means you can enter a 4 digit pin code instead of a password. If you prefer typing a password click 'do this later'.

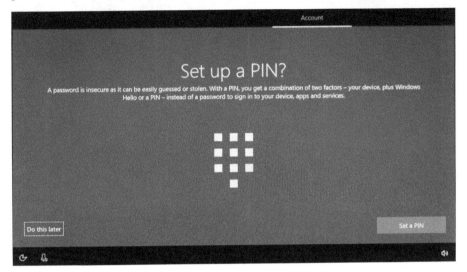

Set up OneDrive

OneDrive is your online storage where you can store your files and access them from any of your devices. Click 'yes' to enable OneDrive.

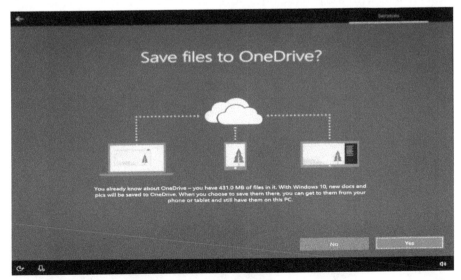

Meet Cortana

Here you can enable your digital assistant and use voice commands.

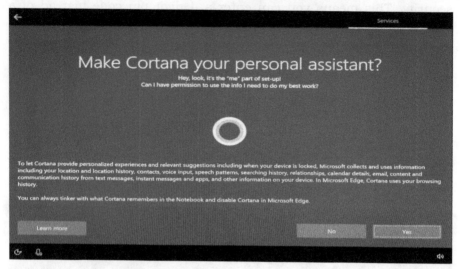

Click 'yes' to enable Cortana, or click 'no' if you can't be bothered talking to your computer.

Privacy Settings

I find it useful to turn the diagnostics to 'basic', turn off 'tailored experiences with diagnostic data' and turn off 'relevant ads'. This helps maximise your privacy and limits data sent to Microsoft.

Once Windows has all your preferences and details, it will configure your computer. Time for a coffee... this will take a while.

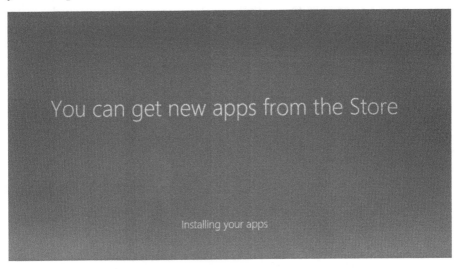

Once the configuration is complete, you'll land on the Windows 10 desktop.

Connecting to a WiFi Network

If you need to connect to another wireless network, you can do so by going to the WiFi settings. Select the WiFi icon on the bottom right of your screen.

Find your WiFi network. This is usually printed on the back of your router.

Click the matching network name in the list.

Click 'connect', then on the next screen, type in your WiFi password. This password is usually also on the back of your router, as shown previously. Type it in and click 'next'.

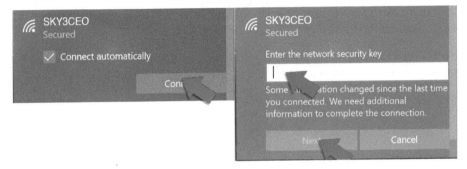

Once Windows has verified your password, it will connect to the network.

It is the same procedure if you are in a coffee shop, library, airport or anywhere else that offers WiFi. Just select their network and ask them for their WiFi details.

Setup your Printer

The exact procedure to installing a printer differs from manufacturer to manufacturer. Each brand comes with its own menu style and software, however the general procedure is the same.

You'll need to install the printer software and drivers. You will need to go to the manufacturer's website to download these.

For HP printers go to

```
support.hp.com/drivers
```

For Canon printers go to

```
www.usa.canon.com/support
```

For Brother printers go to

```
support.brother.com
```

For Epson printers go to

```
www.epson.com/support
```

Somewhere on the manufacturer's website, there will be a product search field. Type in the model name of your printer.

HP Customer Support - Software and Driver Downloads

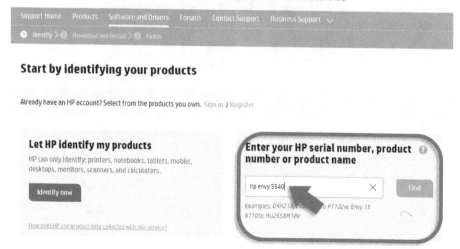

Click 'OK' or 'find'.

From the search results, select your Operating System if required, usually "Windows 10 (64bit)".

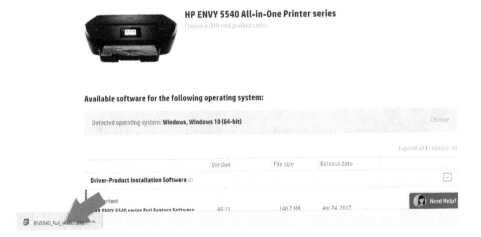

Click on the prompt at the bottom of your browser.

This will run the installation software. Click 'OK' or 'Yes' to the security prompt. If you don't see a prompt, go to your downloads folder in file explorer and double click on the EXE file you just downloaded. Follow the on screen instructions to connect to your printer.

Chapter 3

Getting Around Windows 10

In this chapter we will take a look at the new features, how to get the most out of them and how to use these features of Windows 10 to get your work done.

In the Fall Creator's Update, Microsoft has introduced some enhancements to Windows 10: an App throttling feature that helps Windows to allocate system resources to the apps you are currently using giving less priority to programs that are running in the background.

In addition there is a new People App that allows you to pin your favourite contacts to the task bar, allowing you to drag and drop files and access their contact details quickly.

Onedrive has had an update with an 'on demand' feature, allowing you to have access to all your files but only download the ones you need to your device without having to sync your whole OneDrive.

These are just a few of the new features and we'll take a closer look in this chapter.

The Touch Pad

Laptops come with a built in touch pad that you use your finger to move a pointer on screen to select objects.

Left Click & Right Click

Use the left click button to select objects, double click to open apps or files. Use right click button on files or icons to open context popup menu.

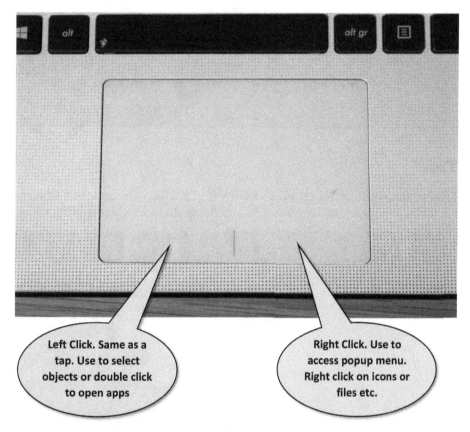

Left Click. Same as a tap. Use to select objects or double click to open apps

Right Click. Use to access popup menu. Right click on icons or files etc.

You can either use the touchpad on the laptop, or you can plug in a mouse if you prefer.

Move Pointer

Slide your finger over the touch pad to move the pointer on the screen. Make sure you keep your finger inside the square.

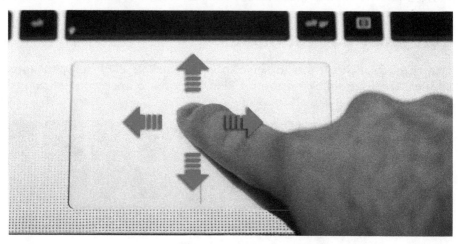

Tap

This is similar to the left click on a mouse. Use this to select objects on the screen. Double tap on icons to open them or start applications.

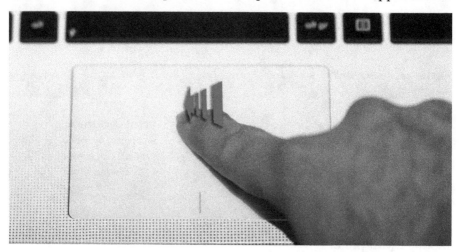

Scroll

Use two fingers on the touch pad to scroll up and down a page, eg on a website.

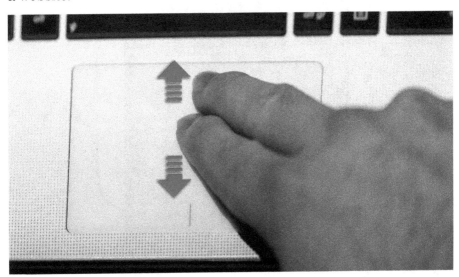

Pinch & Spread

Use your forefinger and thumb on the touch pad to zoom in and out of web pages, images, documents and so on.

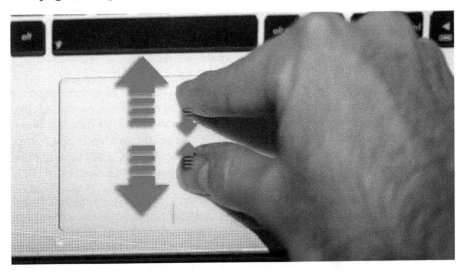

Start Menu

The start menu in Creator's Update has had a few minor enhancements.

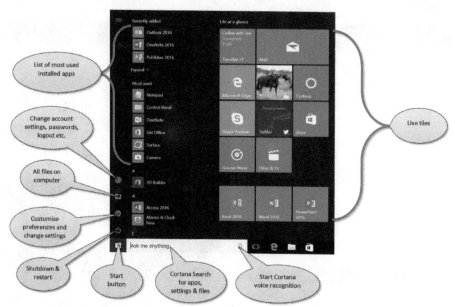

Listed down the far left hand side of your menu you'll see four little icons. From top to bottom, these icons allow you to change your account password or log out, view all files using file explorer, system settings, and shut down.

Also down the left is a list of your most frequently used applications. Underneath this list is an alphabetical list of all apps installed on your system.

On the right hand side of the menu, you'll see coloured tiles representing apps. This is the tile area and these tiles are sometimes called live tiles. Live tiles graphically represent apps and can also display basic notifications such as latest messages, or emails from your mail app, information such as weather, latest news headlines and so on, even when the app isn't running. To run the app you just click on the tile.

The start menu can be displayed as a menu on the bottom left hand side of your screen, and is better suited to point and click desktop users. The start menu can also fill the whole screen, putting more emphasis on the application tiles on the right hand side. This is useful for touch screen users using tablets and phones.

Tile Folders

Introduced in this version of Windows 10 is the ability to group tiles into folders. This can be useful if you have a lot of apps installed on your device. You can start to group your tiles into logical folders; meaning you can group all your communication apps such as facebook, browser, or email, into one folder; all your office apps into another folder and so on.

In this example, I am going to drag all my communication apps into one folder - email, edge, facebook and twitter apps. So choose one of the apps to be the folder: edge browser, then drag the other apps: email, facebook and twitter to this app, as illustrated below.

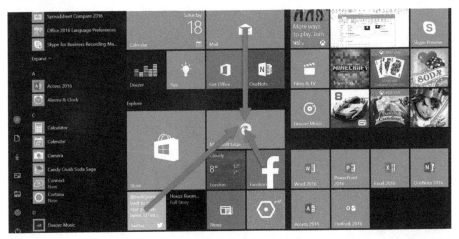

Now all these apps will be grouped into a folder, shown below left. Clicking on the folder will open up your app tiles, shown below right.

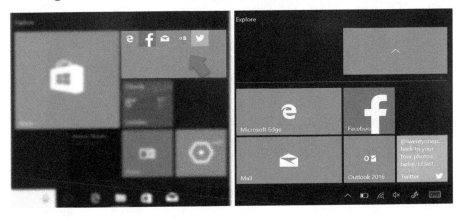

Customising your Start Menu

It is a good idea to customise Windows 10's start menu to your personal preferences and needs. We can do this by arranging, adding and removing tiles on the menu.

Add Tiles to Start Menu

You can add tiles by dragging the icon off the list of apps on the left hand side of the start menu, to the tile section as shown below.

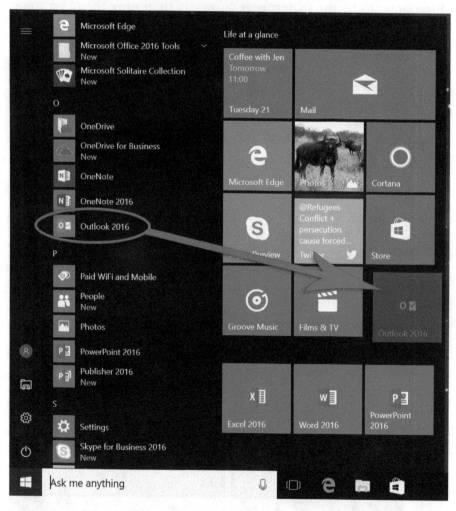

In this way, you can build up a start menu where you can easily access all the apps you use the most, without having to scroll through lists of apps on your start menu.

This is particularly useful if you happen to have a lot of apps installed on your machine.

By doing this, I have built up the following start menu, and created tiles for the apps I use the most by dragging them from the list of apps on the left hand side, into position on the tile area.

This way, you can maximise the use of your machine by removing tiles you don't use or need, keeping and adding tiles for the apps you use the most and grouping them into sections. You can see below, all my Adobe apps are together, and underneath all my Microsoft Office apps.

Also I have access to my calendar; I like to keep up with the news, so I've added the news app; as well as the local weather forecasts, which I find useful.

If the app you want to add to your start menu isn't listed, you can search for it using the search field on your start menu.

In this example I want to add the app called 'wordpad' to the start menu.

I can search for it using the search field. When windows finds the app, it will list it under a heading called 'Apps'.

Right click on the app icon and from the menu that appears select 'pin to start'.

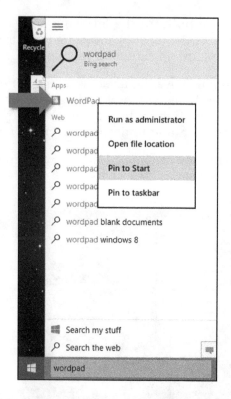

Here you can see, the icon has been pinned as a tile on the start menu. You may have to drag the tile into position.

Move Tiles on the Start Menu

You can move tiles by clicking and dragging them to a new position. The tiles will scroll automatically as you drag your tile up and down the menu.

In the example below, I want to put Outlook 2016 with the rest of the Office 2016 Apps on my start menu. To do this, I just click Outlook 2016 icon, and drag it down to the position where the rest of the Office Apps are.

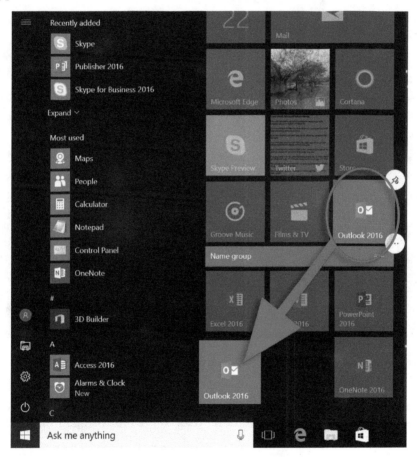

If you are on a touch screen device, tap and hold your finger on the tile for a second, then drag your finger down the screen to the position you want your tile.

Arranging and grouping your tiles like this helps to keep everything organised and easy to find.

Remove Tiles from Start Menu

To remove a tile, right click on it and select the 'unpin icon' that appears on the top right of the tile.

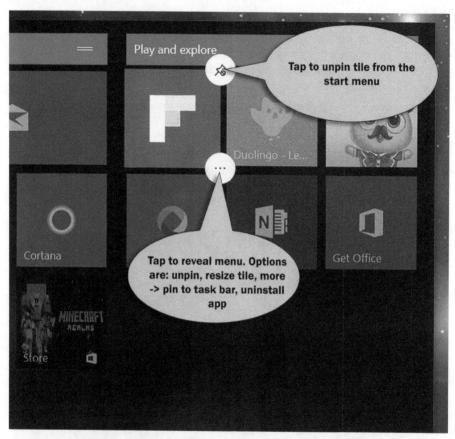

If you are on a touch screen device, tap and hold your finger on the tile until the icons appear.

Windows 10 has a habit of adding tiles you don't use, so it's a good idea to remove all the tiles you don't use, to prevent things from getting too confusing or cluttered.

This will also give you more space to add tiles for the Apps you use all the time, making them more accessible and easy to find.

Resize Tiles on Start Menu

To resize a tile, right click on it. If you are on a touch screen device, tap and hold your finger on the icon to get the icons to appear.

From the two little icons that appear, click the one with the three dots, then from the menu that appears, click resize.

From the slide out menu, click the size you want. You will see that each tile as a number of pre-set sizes.

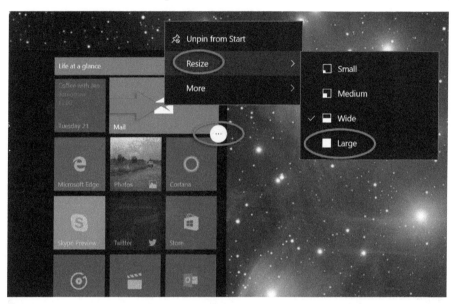

There are usually four sizes to choose from. Small, medium, wide and large. You can see the differences below.

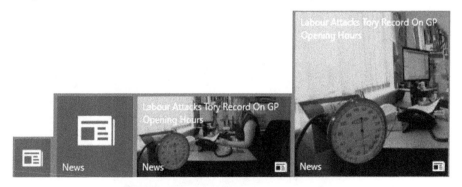

Some app tiles may not have all the sizes available.

Pin Icons to your TaskBar

For more convenience, you can pin all your favourite apps to your task bar along the bottom of your screen.

To do this, right click on the app in the list on the left hand side or on a live tile. Click the icon with the three dots. From the menu that appears, select 'more'.

From the slide out menu select 'pin to taskbar'

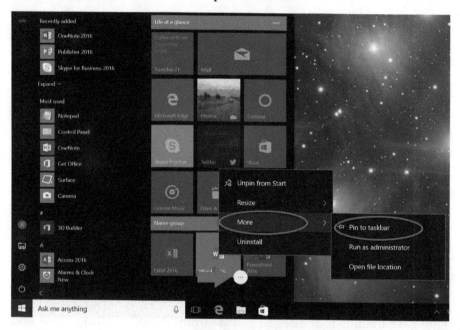

You'll see the icon has been added to your taskbar. If you right click on the icon on your taskbar, you can see a list of recently opened files. Click the little pin icon on the right hand side of the file name to pin the file to the list permanently, if you use that file all the time.

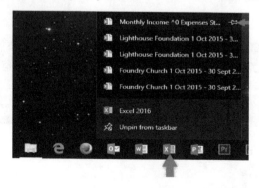

File Explorer

File explorer can be used to find your files on your computer, access your OneDrive, network resources and external hard drives or flash drives. You can find it on your taskbar or on your start menu.

Down the left hand side you will find a list of all the libraries of files on your computer, ie documents, photographs, music and videos.

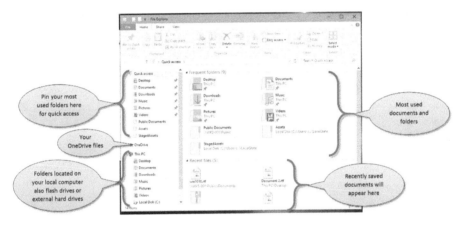

At the top, Windows will start to list the most used libraries you have accessed.

If you click on 'quick access' you will see a list of your most recently accessed files.

Along the top of the explorer window you will see the ribbon menus. Much like the style introduced in Microsoft Office, tools and features are grouped into ribbons.

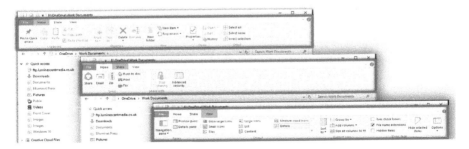

Home Ribbon

On the home ribbon, you'll find all your most common tools, such as copy and paste files, create folders, move files, delete files and show file properties.

Share Ribbon

On the share ribbon you can burn files to a CD, print them, zip them up into a compressed file - useful if you want to email a few documents together. Or you can share files with other computers on your home network or home group if you have one set up.

View Ribbon

With the view ribbon you can display your files as a list, as icons and thumbnails. Icons and thumbnail views can be useful for browsing photographs.

Do this by clicking on the layout options in the middle of the ribbon (large icons, medium sized icons, list or details).

You can also sort files by date added, alphabetically or by size.

Do this by clicking 'sort by'. From the menu, select 'name' to list your files alphabetically by name, or click 'date...' to sort by 'date edited' or 'date created'.

Sharing Files from File Explorer

Share option on right click context menu. Right click on the file you want to share, then from the popup menu, select 'share'.

From the popup dialog box, select the person you want to share the document with. Contacts that you have added to the people app or pinned to your taskbar will appear at the top. If the contact is not in the list, you can send via email or skype at the bottom.

The options will depend on what apps you have installed.

In this example, I am going to email the document. An integrated email will appear in the window allowing you to type a message.

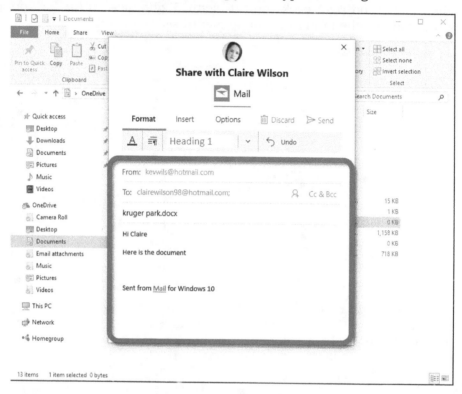

Click 'send' when you're ready to send your email.

Basic File Management

There are many different types of file types; files for photos, videos, documents, speadsheets, presentations and so on. These files are identified by a file extension. So for example...

A photograph is usually saved as a JPEG or JPG. Eg **photo-of-sophie.jpg**. This could be from a graphics package or a camera.

A document is usually saved as a DOC or DOCX. Eg: **production-resume.docx**. This is usually from a word processor such as Microsoft Word.

The 3 or 4 letters after the period is called a file extension and it is what Windows uses to identify the application needed to open the file.

It's best to save all your files into your OneDrive.

Creating Folders

It's a good idea to create folders to help organise all your files. You could have a folder for your personal documents, work documents, presentations, vacation/holiday photos, college work and so on. To do this open your File Explorer.

On the left hand side of your screen, navigate to the place you want to create a folder. In this example, I'm going to create a folder in my 'OneDrive'.

From the home ribbon along the top of your screen, click 'new folder'.

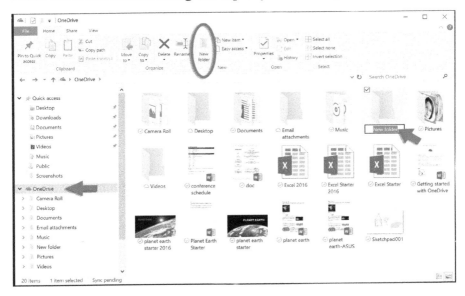

On the right hand side of your screen, you'll see a new folder appear called 'new folder'.

Delete the text 'new folder' and type in a meaningful name - ideally the name of the group of documents you are saving into this folder.

Moving Files

There are a few methods to use when moving or copying files. I prefer the drag and drop method - which seems quicker and easier.

Open your File Explorer

On the left hand side of the window, open up the folder you want to move your file into. In the example below, I am going to move some excel documents into my excel folder. My excel folder is in my documents folder on OneDrive.

So I'm going to click on OneDrive, go down to 'documents' and click on the small down arrow on the left hand side to open the folder. Inside here, you can see the 'excel' folder in the 'documents' folder.

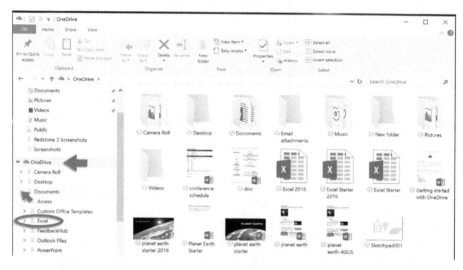

Now click on the folder where the document you want to move is saved. In this example, the file is saved in OneDrive and is called 'excel 2016'. All you need to do is drag and drop the file into the folder, as shown below.

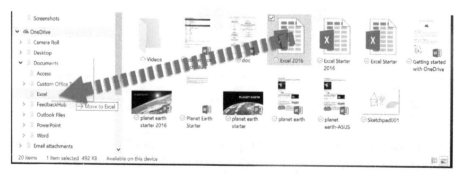

Copying Files

Open your File Explorer

On the left hand side of the window, open up the folder you want to copy your file into. In the example below, I am going to copy an excel document into my excel folder. My excel folder is in my documents folder on OneDrive.

So I'm going to click on OneDrive, go down to 'documents' and click on the small down arrow on the left hand side to open the folder. Inside here, you can see the 'excel' folder in the 'documents' folder.

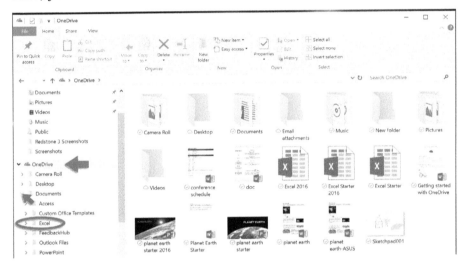

Now click on the folder where the document you want to copy is saved. In this example, the file is saved in OneDrive and is called 'excel Starter 2016'.

All you need to do is hold down the control key (ctrl), then drag and drop the file into the folder, as shown below.

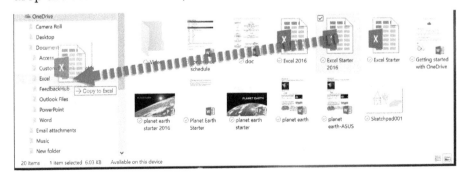

Renaming Files

To rename a file, open up your File Explorer and find the file you want to rename.

Navigate to the folder your file is saved in. In this demo it's in the OneDrive, Documents folder. Click on the file to select it.

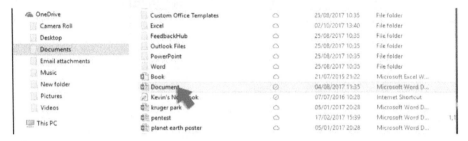

From the home ribbon click 'rename'.

You'll see the name of the file highlighted in blue.

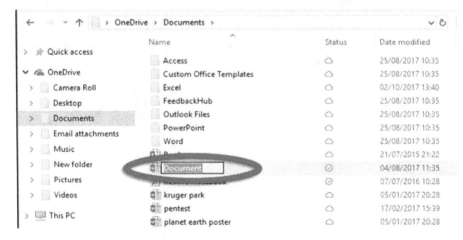

Now type the new name of the file.

External Drives

You can attach storage devices to your computer. The most common ones are memory sticks; also called usb keys, usb sticks, flash drives or thumb drives. The other types are portable hard drives.

Memory sticks are usually smaller in capacity ranging from 1GB all the way up to 256GB. Portable hard drives can be larger than 1TB.

When you plug one of these devices into your computer, the device will show up in File Explorer, under the 'This PC' section.

Double click the drive icon, circled above, to open the contents of the drive.

OneDrive

OneDrive is your cloud file hosting service and synchronises your files between your device (pc, laptop, phone or tablet) and the cloud file hosting service.

You'll find OneDrive in your File Explorer window. OneDrive is where you should save all your files from Microsoft Office, photographs, music, videos and so on. The advantage is, if your computer crashes, you won't lose all your files as they will still be stored on OneDrive.

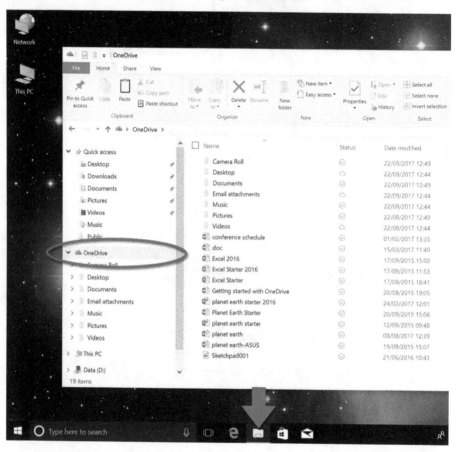

The other advantage of OneDrive, is you can access all your files on all your devices. So you can see your documents on your PC, phone, tablet or laptop, and you can access them from anywhere that has an internet connection.

Files on Demand

Files On-Demand stores all your files on OneDrive Cloud and allows you to open them from Windows File Explorer.

Once you open your file, it is then downloaded to your device. This works with devices that have limited local storage such as tablets and smart phones, that do not have enough space to hold your entire OneDrive contents.

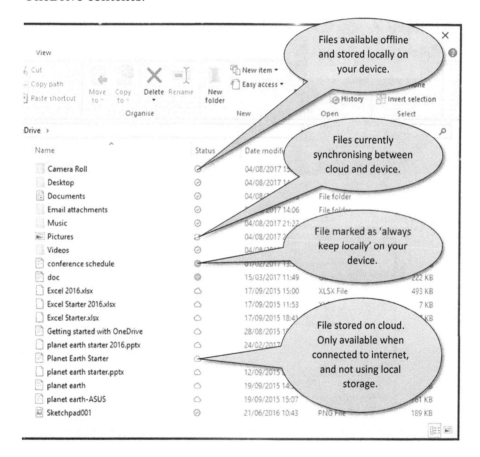

One the icons themselves or in the status column, you'll see some status indicators - as you can see in the illustration above.

Enable and Disable On Demand

Right-click the OneDrive cloud icon in the notification area. From the popup menu select 'settings'.

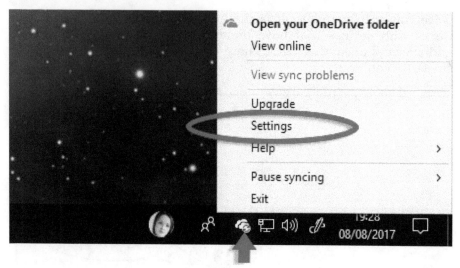

Select the 'settings' tab.

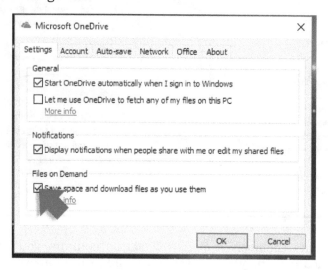

Under 'Files On-Demand', click the tick box next to 'Save space and download files as you use them' to enable the feature.

This will mark all your files as 'online', meaning they are stored on OneDrive Cloud not on your device. When you select a file to open, your file is downloaded to your device and then opened.

Making files available Offline

Having full access to all your files on OneDrive without having do download the whole contents to your device is great, but what happens if you don't always have an internet connection? Well, you can mark certain files as 'available offline', meaning OneDrive will download these files to your device.

To do this, select the files you want to make available offline - hold down control and select your files, if you want more than one.

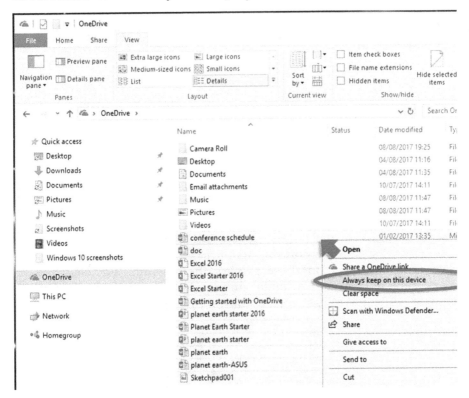

Right click on the selected files and from the popup menu select, 'always keep on this device'.

OneDrive will download the selected files to your device so you can access them when you don't have a connection. If you change your files while offline, OneDrive will sync the changes once you connect to the internet.

Task Bar

The task bar has two new options, one is the Cortana/Windows search box. This allows you to search for anything on your device or ask Cortana a question.

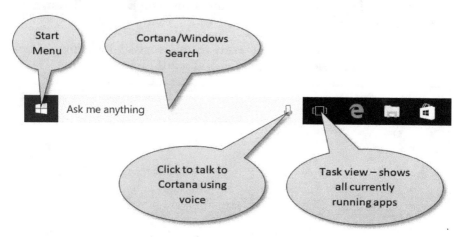

The other button is the task view option that allows you to see currently running apps. This enables you to switch to that app by tapping on its icon or create a new virtual desktop.

On the far right you will see the system tray. This has icons representing wifi networks, volume control, action center, as well as a clock and date. You can click on these to view their details. Eg, click on the clock/time to view your calendar and upcoming events, or click on the volume control to adjust your audio volume.

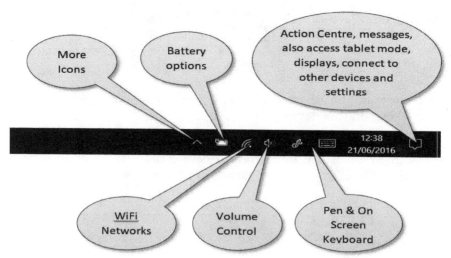

Action Centre

The action centre shows alerts and messages from different applications. You can find action centre by clicking the icon on the bottom right of the task bar, or swiping inwards from the right hand edge of your screen.

These notifications could be email message that have just arrived, system messages or status alerts from applications.

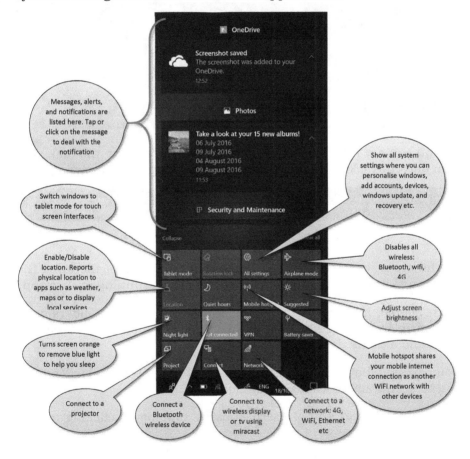

Along the bottom of the notifications window you will see some common settings, eg tablet mode, display settings, media connect for connecting to projectors, second screens etc.

Task View Button

The task view button will show all your currently running apps and display them in thumbnails along the centre of the screen.

As you can see from the screen above, when tapping on the task view icon on your taskbar, a thumbnail list of your apps will appear.

At the top of each thumbnail, you will see the title of the app. The thumbnail itself is a preview of what is currently running in that app.

For example, in this screen, I have music app running, folders open in file explorer, a website open in Edge browser, a blank paint canvas open and a blank document.

You can see what apps are running in the background and will enable you to keep track of what you are doing.

You can switch to any of these apps by tapping or clicking on the thumbnail.

This is called multi tasking.

Using Multiple Desktops

'Multiple desktops' is almost like having two or more desks in your office where you can do your work. You could have a desktop for your web browsing and email, another desktop for your word processing, another desktop for your photo editing and sharing and so on.

Multiple desktops help to organise your tasks together. So you can keep things you are working on together.

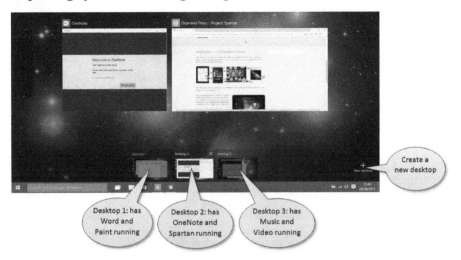

Click on 'new desktop' to open a new desktop, then you can open the apps you want to run.

In this example, open wordpad and paint app. Click the task view button on the task bar, then click 'new desktop'. Now open OneNote and Edge app. Hit the task view button again and click 'new desktop'. Now open groove music and TV & Videos app. So now I have a desktop for my word processing and graphics, a second for my note taking and research with OneNote & Edge, and a third desktop for entertainment.

To get a preview of what is running in a particular desktop, hover your mouse over the thumbnails listed across the bottom of the screen. You will see the large thumbnails along the centre of the screen change. This shows you what is running. To switch to an app click on its thumbnail.

To switch between the desktops, click on the thumbnails listed across the bottom of the screen (desktop 1, desktop 2, desktop 3 and so on). You'll see it's easier to flick between the apps when they are grouped into different desktops for different tasks and projects.

Multiple Screens

You can plug in more than one screen into most modern computers or tablets if you have the correct adapters.

You can set up multiple screens by right clicking on your desktop and selecting 'display settings'.

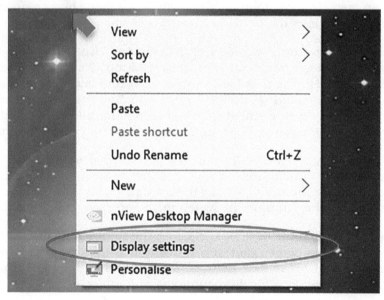

Select 'extend these displays' from the 'multiple displays' drop down menu shown below.

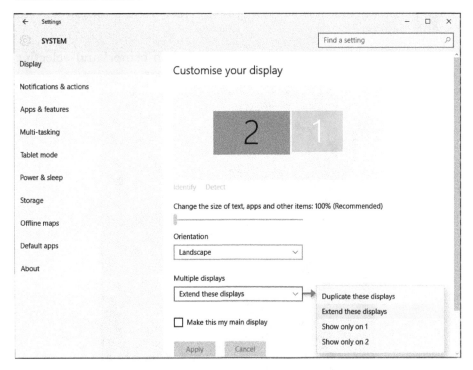

Your screens are identified by a number, shown above. To check which is which, click 'identify' and you'll see a big number appear on each screen.

Make sure you click on your main display using the numbered rectangular icons at the top of the screen. Remembering which number appeared on which screen, click the one you use to do most of your work and click 'make this my main display'. This tells apps that this 'main display' is the one where you will control windows from and do most of your work.

The other display becomes your secondary display; a second desk. This could be another monitor, tv screen or projector.

Using Projectors

Much like using multiple screens, you can also use a projector as your second display.

You can access this by clicking on your 'action center' and selecting 'project'. This will bring up the 'project' side bar.

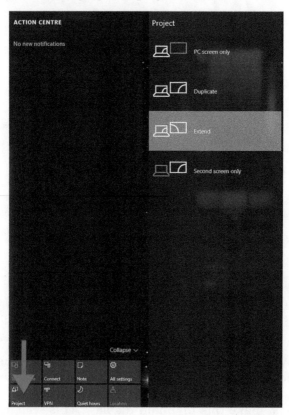

You can also press Windows-P on your keyboard.

Duplicate PC screen onto Second Screen

Everything you do on the laptop screen will be duplicated on the second screen. So both screens will show the same image.

Second Screen Only

This disables your PC's monitor and allows the display to only appear on the second screen.

PC Screen Only

This disables the projector and allows the information to be seen only on the PC's monitor.

<u>Extend</u> PC screen onto Second Screen

The second screen acts as an extension to your laptop screen rather than just a duplicate. So you can have something on your laptop screen and show different images on the projector.

This allows you to move windows from the laptop's screen (screen 1) to the second screen and vice versa.

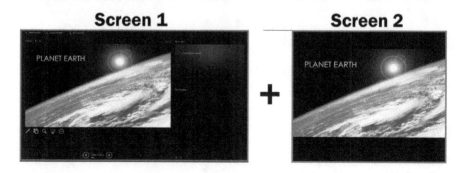

Your second screen becomes an extension to your laptop's screen (screen 1).

Using Continuum

Windows 10 is designed to run seamlessly on all your devices. Whether you are using a phone, tablet, xbox, laptop/notebook or desktop PC, Windows 10 will automatically select the correct mode for your phone or tablet with a touch screen interface or a desktop/laptop PC with a point and click interface.

Desktop PC/Laptop

Windows 10 is capable of running on a full sized desktop computer or workstation and runs in a similar way to Windows 7 did back in its day, with mouse, keyboard and the start menu available to access your files and programs. This is desktop mode.

Tablets

Tablet mode is tailored to smaller screens and touch interfaces. So instead of a keyboard and mouse, you tap on the icons on the screen with your finger. To make this easer, icons are larger and apps run full screen.

Chapter 3: Getting Around Windows 10

For convertible devices, such as the Surface, there are two modes, tablet and desktop.

When using the device as a tablet, Windows 10 will automatically change to tablet mode which is more touch-friendly.

Once you connect a mouse and keyboard, or flip your laptop around, Windows will go into desktop mode. Apps turn back into desktop windows that are easier to move around with a mouse and you'll see your desktop again.

For Phones

Another new feature of Continuum is the ability to use your phone as if it were a PC. However, this only works on Lumia phones and requires a purchase of a display dock. You will need to connect a keyboard, mouse and monitor to the dock.

Just plug your phone into the dock and you can use your apps as if you were using your PC or connect to projectors to present. This way you always have your files with you.

Arranging Windows on Desktop

It's useful when working in Windows 10 to arrange the windows on your desktop, especially when you're using more than one application at a time. For example, you could be browsing the web and writing a Word document at the same time- perhaps you're researching something, you could have Word open and your web browser next to it on the screen.

Lets take a look at moving and resizing widows on the desktop.

Moving a Window

Move your mouse pointer to the top of the window.

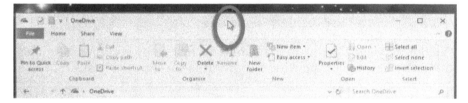

Now click and drag the window to your desired position on the screen.

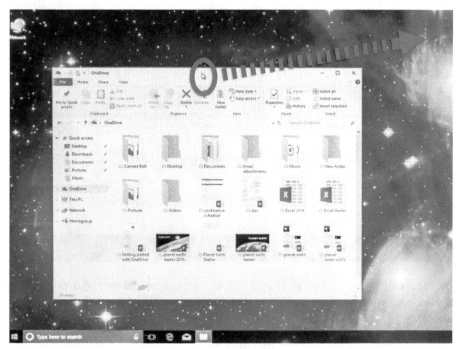

Resizing a Window

To resize a window, move your mouse pointer to the bottom right corner of the window - your pointer should turn into a double edged arrow.

The double edged arrow means you can resize the window. Now click and drag the edge of the window until it is the size you want.

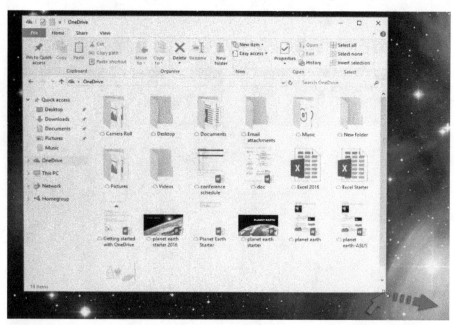

You can drag any edge of the window - left, bottom or right edge, but I find using the corner allows you to freely resize the window much more easily.

If you're on a touch screen, tap and drag the corner of the window.

Minimise, Maximise & Close a Window

On the top right hand side of every window, you'll see three icons. You can use these icons to minimise a window, ie reduce it to the taskbar essentially hiding the window from the desktop. With the second icon, you can maximise the window so it fills the entire screen, or if the window is already maximised, using the same icon, restore the window to its original size, and the third icon you can use to close a window completely.

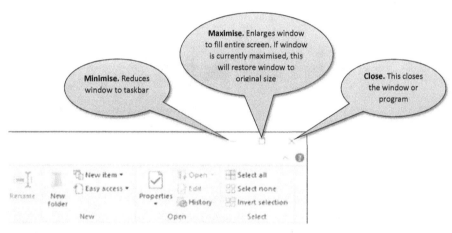

Using Windows Side by Side

Using the move and resize window skills covered earlier, you can arrange your windows on your desktop.

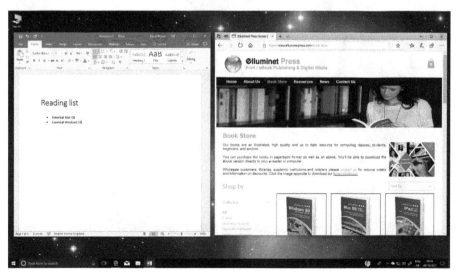

Window Snap Feature

You can now have four apps snapped on the same screen with a new quadrant layout.

Windows will also show other apps and programs running for additional snapping and even make smart suggestions on filling available screen space with other open apps.

Click and drag the window to the right edge of the screen until your mouse pointer is on the edge and you see a translucent box appear on the right hand half of the screen.

Keyboard Shortcuts

Keyboard shortcuts are performed using 3 main function keys: the control key, the windows key and the alt key.

To execute a command using a keyboard shortcut. Hold down the appropriate function key and tap the key for the function you want shown in the table below.

Windows + Tab	Opens thumbnail list of open applications
Windows + A	Open Windows 10 notification centre
Windows + D	Show Windows desktop
Windows + E	Open Windows Explorer
Windows + K	Connect to wireless displays and audio devices
Windows + P	Project a screen
Windows + R	Run a command
Windows + X	Open Start button context menu
Windows key + Arrow key	Snap app windows left, right, corners, maximize, or minimize
Windows key + Comma	Temporarily peek at the desktop
Windows Key	Show windows start menu
Alt + Tab	Switch to previous window
Alt + Space	Reveals drop down menu on current window: Restore, move, size, minimize, maximize or close.
Alt + F4	Close current app
Ctrl + Shift + Esc	Open Task Manager
Ctrl + Z	Undo Command
Ctrl + X	Cut selected text
Ctrl + C	Copy selected text
Ctrl + V	Paste selected text at cursor position
Ctrl + P	Print

Other Features

Other features worth noting are the Dynamic Lock, Storage Sense, Blue Light Reduction and App Throttling.

Dynamic Lock

Before activating the dynamic lock, you will first need to pair your device or phone with your PC or laptop via Bluetooth. To activate dynamic lock go to...

Settings App -> Accounts -> Sign-in Options -> Dynamic Lock

Tick the box next to 'Allow Windows to detect when you're away and automatically lock the device.'

Storage Sense

Over time, temporary files, caches and files in the recycle bin start to accumulate. Storage sense monitors and deletes these files, keeping your system running smoothly. This feature is disabled by default but you can enable it easily from the Settings App.

Settings App -> System -> Storage -> Storage Sense

Switch the slider to 'on'. Click 'change how we free up space'. Turn both options to 'on'.

Click 'clean now' to manually run the "temporary file" clean-up.

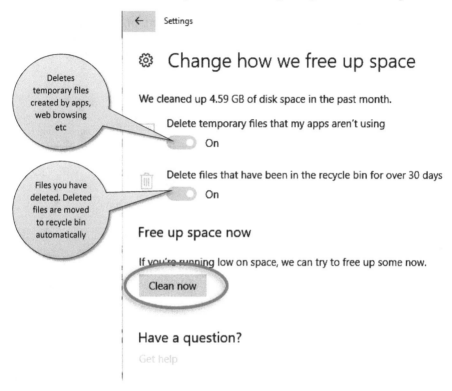

When you turn the two sliders to 'on', Windows will automatically clear temporary files and empty the recycle bin during its maintenance schedule, so this feature can work silently in the background and you don't have to worry about it.

Blue Light Reduction

This feature is designed to reduce the amount of blue light emitted from your device's screen in the evenings, which is said to suppress the secretion of melatonin in the brain affecting your ability to sleep. To turn it on, go to...

Settings App -> System -> Display -> Night Light.

Switch the slider to 'on' then click 'night light settings'.

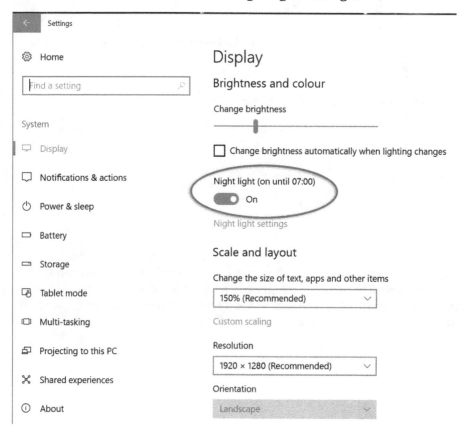

Click 'turn on now'. You can adjust the level of the night light using the 'colour temperature at night' slider.

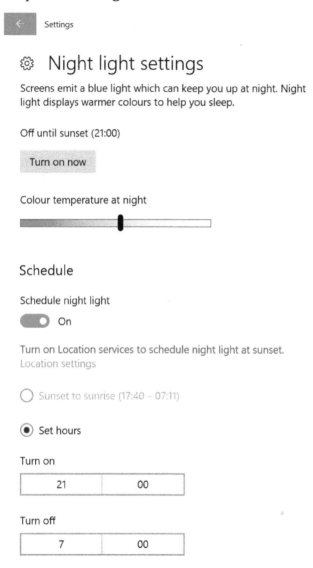

If you want the night light to come on at a specific time each night, shift the 'schedule night light' slider to 'on' and enter the time in the 'turn on' field and the time to turn it off in the 'turn off' field.

You'll see the screen turn an orange colour. Any work you do; printing, editing, photos etc will not have the orange tint.

App Power Throttling

This feature reduces resources such as CPU time and memory used by apps and services running in the background, so that more of your computer's resources are devoted to tasks you're currently working on in the foreground.

This feature can be particularly useful if you are running games, apps that require a lot of processing power, or running apps on a machine that is older with limited resources.

You will be able to see which apps have been throttled in Task Manager. To open your Task Manager, right click on your task bar and from the popup menu select 'task manager'. You may need to click 'more details' to expand the window.

Click the 'details' tab and you'll see a list of processes and some details about each process. In the status column you'll see 'running', 'suspended' or 'throttled'.

Name	PID	Status	User name	CPU	Memory (p...	Description
svchost.exe	2744	Throttled		00	1,716 K	Svchost
svchost.exe	2792	Throttled		00	5,560 K	Svchost
svchost.exe	3652	Throttled		00	5,456 K	Svchost
svchost.exe	3556	Throttled		00	3,720 K	Svchost
svchost.exe	4868	Throttled	kevwi	00	6,660 K	Host Process for Windows Services
System	4	Running	SYSTEM	00	28 K	NT Kernel & System
System Idle Process	0	Running	SYSTEM	99	4 K	Percentage of time the processor is idle
System interrupts	-	Running	SYSTEM	00	0 K	Deferred procedure calls and interrupt ser...
SystemSettings.exe	8652	Suspended	kevwi	00	268 K	Settings
SystemSettingsBroke...	10444	Running	kevwi	00	1,956 K	System Settings Broker
taskhostw.exe	4952	Running	kevwi	00	4,396 K	Host Process for Windows Tasks
Taskmgr.exe	8676	Running	kevwi	00	13,552 K	Task Manager
Video.UI.exe	9624	Suspended	kevwi	00	220 K	Video Application
vmcompute.exe	3408	Running		00	1,332 K	Vmcompute
vmms.exe	2864	Running		00	7,184 K	Vmms
wininit.exe	884	Running		00	800 K	Wininit
winlogon.exe	984	Running		00	1,336 K	Winlogon
WinStore.App.exe	10912	Suspended	kevwi	00	284 K	Store
WINWORD.EXE	10008	Running	kevwi	00	31,516 K	Microsoft Word
wmpnetwk.exe	200	Running		00	2,100 K	Wmpnetwk
WUDFHost.exe	1592	Running		00	1,388 K	WUDFHost
WUDFHost.exe	1900	Running		00	1,372 K	WUDFHost

Pairing Devices with Bluetooth

On your Phone or device go to action centre and tap bluetooth, make sure it's turned on.

On your PC/Laptop go to

Settings App -> Devices -> Bluetooth

Shift the Bluetooth slider to 'on'. When you turn on your Bluetooth, your laptop or PC will start scanning for other Bluetooth devices such as your phone and list them in this window.

Click on the device you want to pair with and click 'pair', in this example the device is called 'WinPhone'. You'll see a randomly generated passcode pop up in a dialog box.

Type this code into the prompt on your phone and hit OK. Some devices won't need a passcode such as headphones, pens, mice and some keyboards.

Cortana Personal Assistant

Cortana is Microsoft's voice activated, personal assistant. You can use Cortana to set reminders using your natural voice rather than typing or clicking an icon.

You can ask Cortana questions about current weather and traffic conditions, local points of interest such as closest or popular places to eat, you can find sports scores and biographies.

You can find Cortana by clicking in the search field on the task bar. Once you do that, her window will appear.

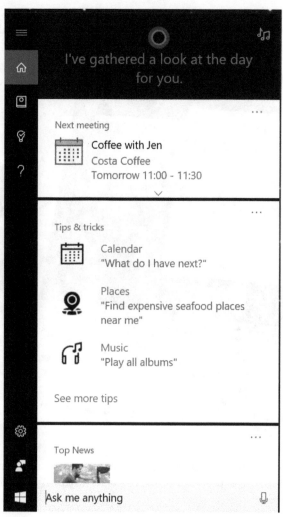

Using Cortana

Tap/Click the microphone icon, located on the right hand side of the search field on the task bar.

If you have it enabled, you can also get Cortana's attention by saying, "Hey Cortana!"

To enable this feature, tap in Cortana's search field 'ask me anything', tap the settings icon, and turn the slider to 'on' under 'hey cortana'.

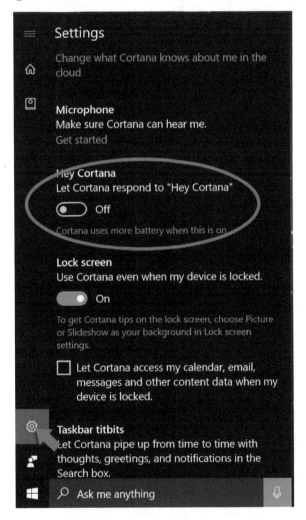

Now whenever you need Cortana, just say "Hey Cortana!" or tap the mic icon in the 'ask me anything' field and ask her a question.

Once you have gotten Cortana's attention, she will start listening to what you say. You'll see something like this. Notice the word 'listening' in the search field.

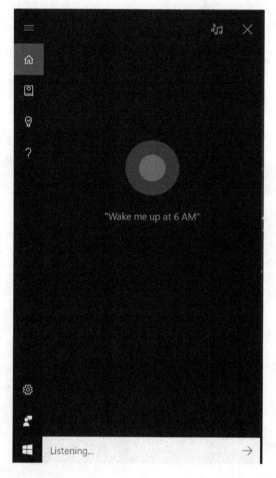

Try some of the following voice commands. You may need to change some of the names.

- *"Call Sister at home"*
- *"Send text to Sophie: When are you coming to play?"*
- *"Create a meeting with Claire at 2pm tomorrow"*
- *"Make Note: Pick up kids, take dog for walk, feed kids, buy milk and ice-cream on way home"*
- *"Show me restaurants nearby"*
- *"What's the forecast for this weekend?"*
- *"How do I get to Liverpool One?" or "Show me directions to Liverpool One."*

Other Features

Cortana also has some extra options located on the tool bar down the left hand side of the window.

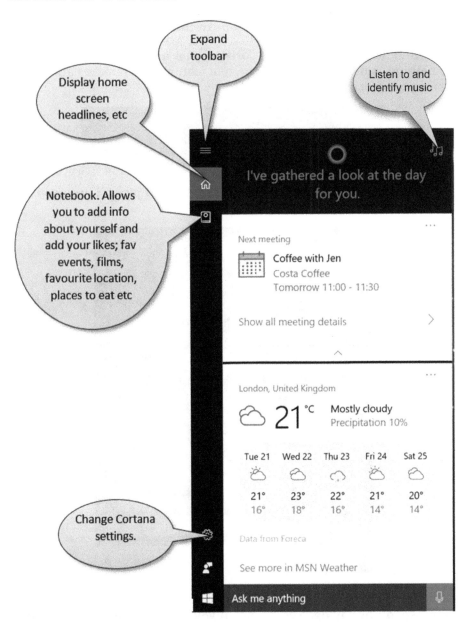

Expand toolbar

Display home screen headlines, etc

Listen to and identify music

Notebook. Allows you to add info about yourself and add your likes; fav events, films, favourite location, places to eat etc

Change Cortana settings.

I've gathered a look at the day for you.

Next meeting

Coffee with Jen
Costa Coffee
Tomorrow 11:00 - 11:30

Show all meeting details

London, United Kingdom

21 °C   Mostly cloudy
        Precipitation 10%

Tue 21	Wed 22	Thu 23	Fri 24	Sat 25
21°	23°	22°	21°	20°
16°	18°	16°	14°	14°

Data from Foreca

See more in MSN Weather

Ask me anything

Notebook is Cortana's book of information about you. You can add and edit areas of interest from your daily routine, news and headlines, music, weather, food, lifestyle and so on. Tap the notebook icon on the tool bar and scroll through the categories: eat & drink, events, films & TV etc. Edit the details according to your personal tastes, for example, add Chinese or Italian favourite foods in the 'Eat & Drink' section.

You can add reminders using Cortana, just ask her to remind you of something, simply by tapping the mic icon on the taskbar and say it using your voice.

Try something like: "Hey Cortana, remind me to pick Claire up today at 4:30pm."

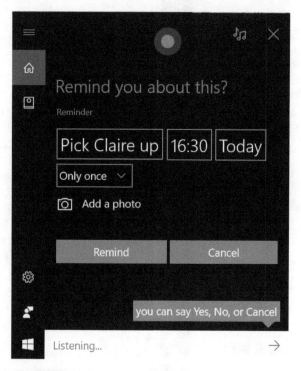

Cortana will confirm your reminder and ask you if it sounds good. You can respond by saying, 'yes' or 'no'. If you say 'yes', she will store your reminder in your reminders list. If you say 'no', she will ask you what you want to change; reminder, date or time. Change them by speaking the word, then speaking the amendment.

With Cortana music, she can identify music playing just by listening. She will then search for it. Can be a useful feature if you hear a song and what to know what it is or where you can get a copy.

Just tap the music icon on the tool bar and she begins listening...

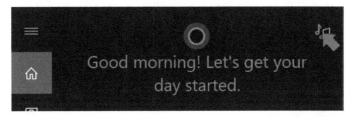

If Cortana knows the song, she'll find it for you.

You can tap or click on this song to purchase a copy from the App Store.

Customise Cortana

You can customise Cortana in the settings pane.

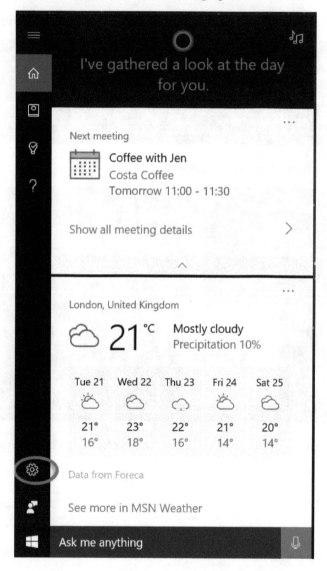

To do this, click the settings icon on the tool bar circled above.

From here you can change your name and set different preferences. You can turn Cortana off or on, if you'd rather not use voice.

Scroll down the rest of the settings, and adjust them accordingly.

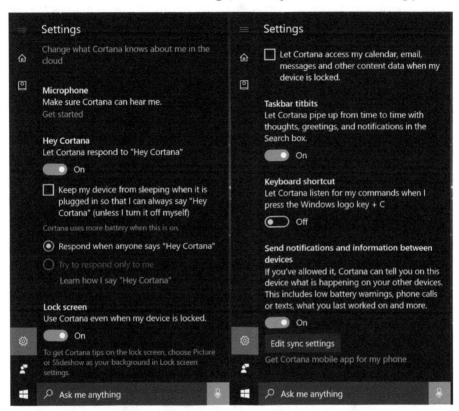

The functions are pretty well explained on the settings page, so have a read through.

A few things worth noting. If you're having a few issues with Cortana not hearing you, tap 'get started' under 'microphone' and run through the mic settings to make sure Cortana is receiving an audio signal.

For additional security and to prevent Cortana responding to anyone, you can train Cortana to respond to you only. Tap "learn how to 'say Hey Cortana!'" Then tap 'start' to run through the test phrases. You might need to tap the mic icon on the search bar if she isn't picking up your voice.

It's not advisable to allow Cortana to access calendar, email or messages when your device is locked - could be a security risk if someone else gets hold of your phone.

Sending notifications and info between devices is handy if you have a Windows phone, tablet and or a PC. If for example you receive a text or phone call and you're working on your PC and don't hear your phone ring, a notification will pop up on your PC informing you.

You might want to adjust the SafeSearch settings, this filters out pornography, suicide/self harm, drugs, criminal and malicious content. Either set to 'moderate' or 'strict'. This also helps to keep Cortana from returning potentially unsafe websites.

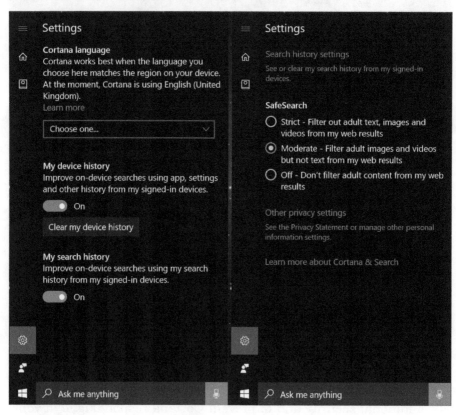

Most of them you probably won't have to change much.

Chapter 4

Internet, Email & Communication

Windows 10 has a new web browser called Edge and is installed by default. It has new features that allow you to annotate websites, share and make notes.

We'll also take a brief look at two other browsers, Google Chrome and FireFox. These are a good alternative to Microsoft Edge.

Windows 10 also has revamped mail and calendar apps, where you can add all your email accounts, whether it be Google, Yahoo, Microsoft account or any other account and have them all in one place.

We'll take a look at these later in this chapter. Also we'll take a look at how to get started using Skype for making calls.

Lets begin by taking a look at Microsoft's new browser, Edge.

Microsoft Edge Web Browser

Codenamed "Spartan", Microsoft Edge is built for the modern web, is a more lightweight web browser and replaces Internet Explorer in Windows 10 and has had a few tweaks in the Creator's Update.

It no longer supports ActiveX controls which makes it a little more secure and integrates with Cortana assistant and OneDrive, it also has annotation tools, reading modes and sharing tools.

Microsoft has also introduced a new icon for the Edge Browser. You can find the icon either on your task bar or on your start menu.

Lets take a look at what Edge looks like. Edge has a cleaner interface than Internet Explorer.

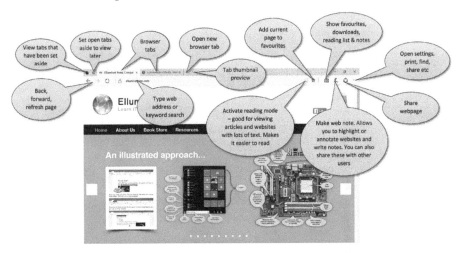

Along the top of the window you will find your address bar where you can enter search keywords or website addresses.

You can add websites to favourites, show favourites, make annotations on web pages, both handwritten or typed.

You can access all these features by tapping or clicking on the icons on your tool bar at the top of the screen.

Bookmarks

You can quickly bookmark the page you are on by clicking on the star icon on the tool bar.

In the dialog box that appears type in a name for the website and select 'choose and item' under 'create in'. Select 'favourites'.

You can also create folders to organise your favourites. Click on 'create new folder' and enter a name in the 'folder name' field.

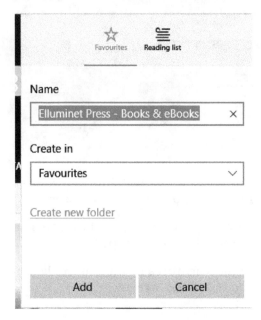

100

Now when you bookmark any site, click 'choose an item' under the 'create in' field and you will be able to select the folder you created. This will allow you to organise your bookmarks into groups.

To revisit your bookmarked sites, click your favourites list icon (circled below).

In the drop down menu, circled below, you can tap the star to view your favourites/bookmarks.

This will open your favourites list. You'll see the website you bookmarked appear at the bottom of the list.

You can drag the websites up and down in the list, to reorder them; or you can drag them into the yellow folders. To create a new yellow folder, right click on the favourites sidebar and from the popup menu select 'create new folder' then type in name.

The 'favourites bar' appears along the top of your Edge browser underneath the navigation buttons and the address bar. This is the place to put all the websites you visit most often.

By default, this bar is hidden, but you can turn it on quite easily. Tap the three dots on the top right, then tap settings. From the settings menu, go down to 'show the favourites bar'. Switch this to 'on'.

Annotations & Notes

You can enter annotation mode by clicking on the icon on the tool bar

You will notice a new tool bar appears along the top of your screen.

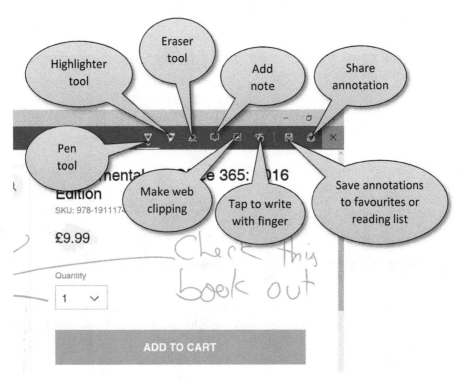

Starting from the left hand side of the tool bar, you have a pen tool.

The next icon across is a highlighter pen.

An eraser tool that allows you to rub out annotations you have drawn.

A note tool that allows you to type annotations in if you can't had write them.

A web clipping tool that allows you to copy a section of the webpage including your annotations to the clipboard where you can paste into a word processing or note taking application.

Pen Tool

Select the pen tool with your mouse or finger/stylus (if using touch interface), then select a colour and pen thickness (size).

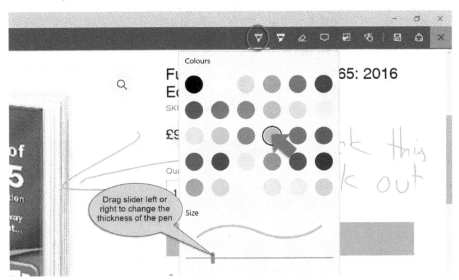

Draw directly on the web page as illustrated below.

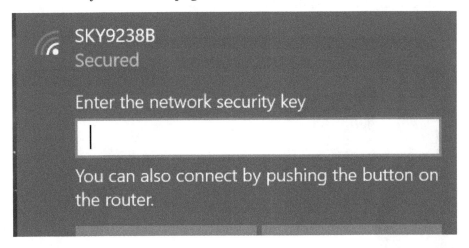

You can highlight headings, draw arrows or handwrite text when doing research for example. Or perhaps you want to highlight a part of a webpage you found useful so it's easier to find when you come back to it. You can save these annotations to your favourites or send them to friends.

Highlighter Pen

Use the highlighter tool to highlight different words or paragraphs on the web page.

Click on a colour in a colour pallet along the top of the drop-down, then use the slider underneath to adjust the size; drag left to make smaller, drag right to make larger.

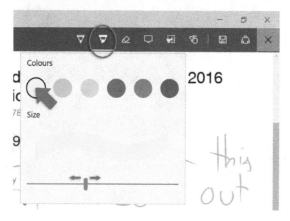

You can draw directly on the screen with your finger or stylus to highlight any text as shown below

There is also an eraser tool so you can rub out any annotations you have made.

Typed Notes

You can also add typed notes with the next icon across. Tap on the note icon, then tap on the webpage, where you want the note to point to.

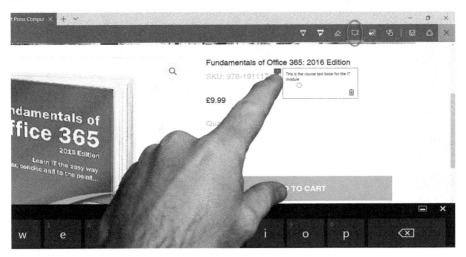

Then type your notes in the text box that appears, either using the on screen keyboard or an attached keyboard. I find attached keyboards easier to type on

Saving Notes

You can save or share all these annotations using the two icons on the right hand side of the tool bar.

Use the first icon to save the annotations into your favourites or reading list. You can also use the second icon to share your annotated web page via email, print it out etc.

Reading Mode

Some websites, especially those with a lot of text can be difficult to print or read on screen.

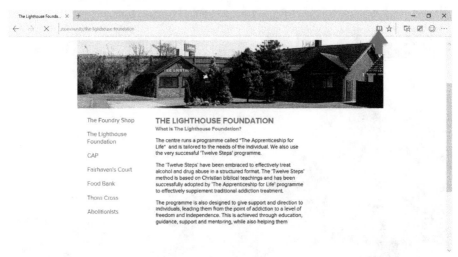

Edge has a reading mode that can be quite useful when reading articles on websites.

Also some websites do not print particularly well since they are designed to be viewed on screen. So by using the reading mode you can print your website article in a more printer friendly fashion.

More Options

There are some hidden menu options in Edge that you can access by clicking on the 3 dots on the far right hand side of the screen. This will reveal a drop down menu

From the menu, you can print the current page, make the text bigger using the zoom function.

You can share the current web page via email or social media by clicking 'share'.

You can search for a particular word on the current web page by clicking 'find on page'.

You can print the current page.

You can adjust settings such as security and privacy.

Print a Page

You can print the current web page by clicking 'print' from the 'more options' icon indicated below.

If you click print from the menu, you will see another dialog box appear asking you what printer you want to print to and number of copies etc.

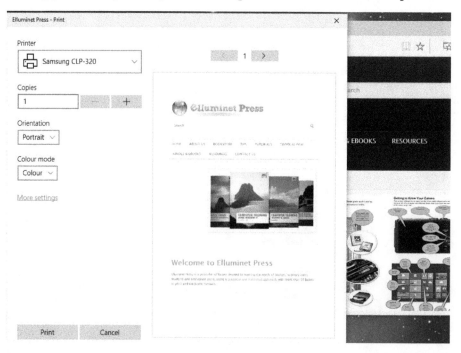

Select the printer from the printer box, enter number of copies if needed.

You can also print portrait or landscape

Select colour mode or black and white

Click print when you are happy with the preview of the printed page shown on the right hand side.

Pin a Website to the Start Menu

A useful feature of Microsoft Edge is the ability to pin a website shortcut onto your start menu.

To do this, you need to open the website in Microsoft Edge. In this example, I am going to add Google Maps, as it's a website I use quite often for travel and finding directions.

Click the icon with the three dots, on the top right of your window.

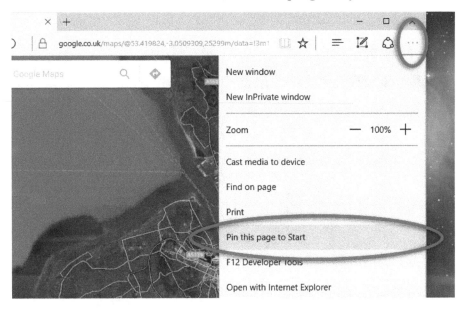

From the drop down menu, select 'pin this page to start'. Click 'yes' to the question 'do you want to pin this tile to start'.

You will find your web page appear as a tile on the start menu. It usually has the Microsoft Edge logo with the name of the website underneath, as shown below.

Pin Website to TaskBar

A useful feature of Microsoft Edge is the ability to pin a website shortcut onto your taskbar. You should only really use this feature for websites you visit very often, as you can quite easily fill up your taskbar with clutter. Perhaps if you use a web based email or facebook - create a taskbar short cut.

To do this, open the website you want to pin in Microsoft Edge.

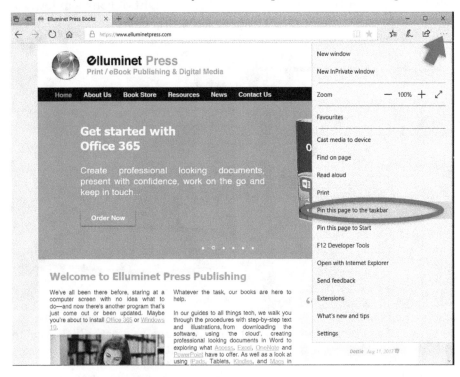

You'll see the website link appear on your task bar. The icon depends on the website's own icon.

Change your Start Page

It's useful to change the start page to automatically go to a page you use most often. Google search is a popular option.

To change the start page, click the 'more options' icon on the top right of your screen. From the menu, select 'settings'.

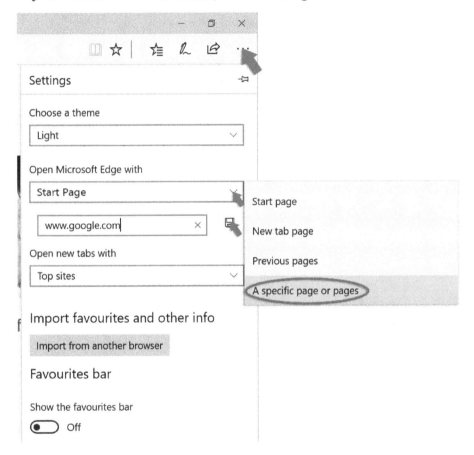

Go down and click on the drop down box that says 'start page'. From the menu select 'a specific page or pages'.

In the 'enter a url' field, type in the web address of the website. In this example I am going to add Google search.

```
www.google.com
```

111

Tab Preview Bar

The tab preview bar gives you a thumbnail preview of the webpage currently open on that tab.

To preview your open website tabs, click the tab preview icon to the right of the tab list, as shown below.

The tab bar will expand to show you a preview of your currently open website tabs.

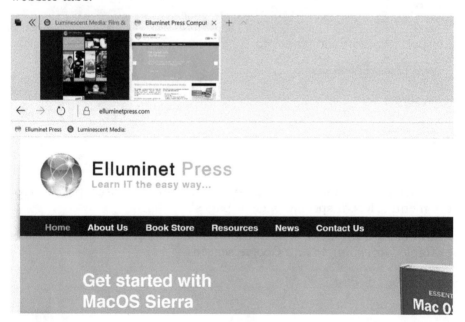

Click on these tabs to switch to that website.

Set Aside Tabs

Microsoft Edge browser opens websites up in tabs. This feature allows you set aside website tabs you have open, so you can restore and look at them later. This helps to avoid visual clutter if you happen to open lots of tabs at the same time.

To set aside open website tabs, click the 'set aside' icon on the top left of your screen.

You'll see all your open website tabs disappear and a new blank website tab open up. This is almost like putting sites 'on the shelf' to look at later.

To view the website tabs you have set aside, click the icon on the top left of your screen to open the sidebar.

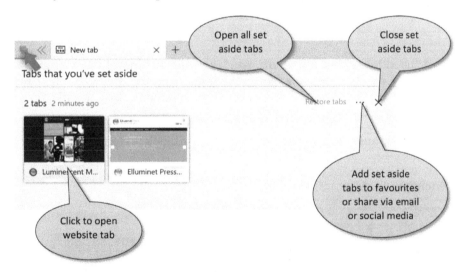

In the sidebar that opens you'll see a list of thumbnail previews of the website tabs you have set aside. Click on these to go back to the website.

Click the three dot icon on the right hand side. From the drop down, you can share the tabs via email or social media, or you can add them to your favourites.

Edge Extensions

Extensions add functionality to the Edge Browser.

To add extensions to Edge, click the 'more' icon on the top right of your screen and select 'extensions'.

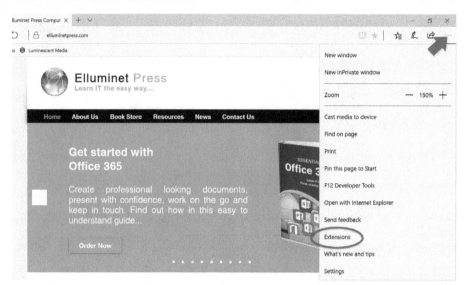

From the sidebar that opens up, you'll see all your installed extensions. To get new extensions click 'get extensions from the store'. At the time of writing there are only a few extensions available, but the library is expected to grow over time.

In this example, I'm going to add the Adblock extension. So click 'AdBlock'.

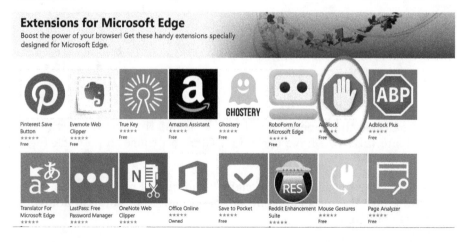

From the extension details page, click 'get'.

AdBlock

BetaFish

★★★☆☆ 91

This product needs to be installed on your internal hard drive.

Free

Get

+ This product is an extension for: Microsoft Edge

The extension will start to download. Once it has installed, click 'launch'.

AdBlock

BetaFish

★★★☆☆ 91

This product is installed.

Launch

+ This product is an extension for: Microsoft Edge

You'll see a prompt telling you there is a new extension, click 'turn on' to enable it.

You can access your extensions anytime, just click the 'more' icon on the top right of your screen and select 'extensions' from the menu. Click on the extension name to change its settings.

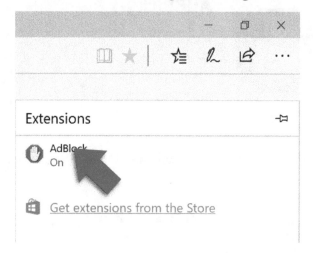

Here, you can enable/disable the extension and if you click 'options', you'll see a webpage with some preferences you can adjust.

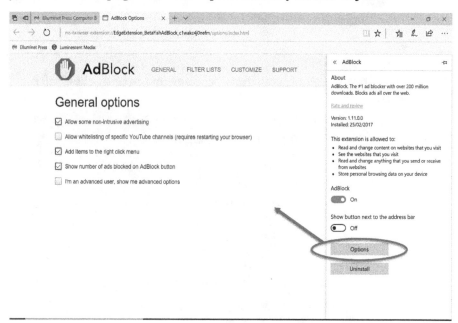

To completely remove the extension just click 'uninstall'.

Web Payments & Microsoft Wallet

Microsoft Wallet is Microsoft's answer to Apple Pay and will be available on Windows 10 Phones. Just look for the icon on your start screen.

You can pay for things with your Microsoft Wallet anywhere you see the contactless symbol or Microsoft Wallet logo.

If this is the first time you're running Wallet, tap 'Sounds good! Sign in' then enter your Microsoft Account email address and password.

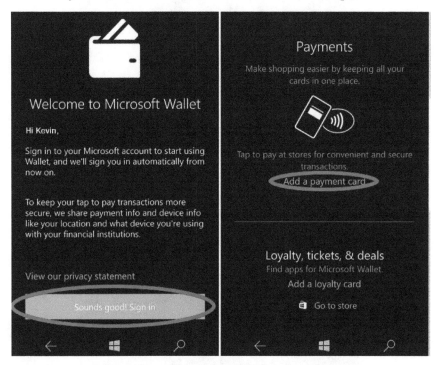

You can add your cards to your Microsoft Wallet by scanning them with your phone's on-board camera. To do this, on the next screen tap 'add a payment card'

117

Tap 'scan your card'.

Now, position your card in the frame as shown below.

Tap screen to capture your card.

Once the card has been captured, run through the process to verify your card. You'll need to enter the security code from the back of your card when prompted.

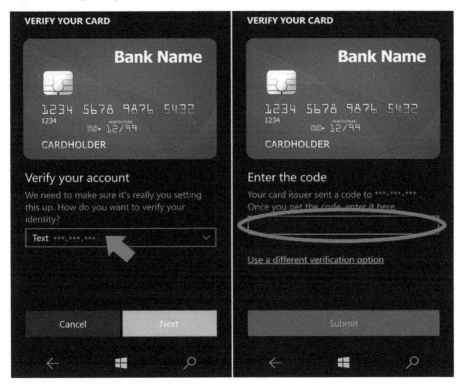

Select a verification method. This is usually via text message to a phone registered to your Microsoft Account. You can also use to send it to your Microsoft Account email address. Tap 'Next'.

Enter the code sent to your phone and tap 'submit'.

Tap 'go to my cards'.

Now when you're in any participating store, launch your wallet, select a card and hold your phone next to the card reader.

Other Browsers Worth Noting

There are a few other browsers that are worth taking note of. These are Google Chrome and FireFox. I prefer Chrome personally but why not give them both a try. Either of these two browsers make great alternatives to Microsoft Edge.

Google Chrome

Google Chrome is a fast and streamlined browser and gives access to its App Store so you can run Google Apps on your browser, connect to Google Drive, edit and save documents using Google's word processor, spreadsheet and presentation apps as well as browsing the web using Google itself.

You can download Google Chrome from

www.google.com/chrome/browser

Hit the download button. Click 'accept and install'. Go to your downloads folder and double click 'chromesetup.exe'

Follow the on screen instructions to install the browser.

Once Chrome has loaded, click the profile icon on the top right and enter your Google account username and password.

This is the same account that you use for Gmail if you have one.

You can use Chrome without a Google account, but you won't get any of the personalised features or be able to add apps to Chrome from the Chrome Store.

FireFox

FireFox is a free browser developed by the Mozilla Corporation and is fast and secure.

You can download FireFox from

`www.firefox.com`

Hit the 'free download' button.

Click 'run', if prompted by your browser.

If you don't get a prompt, go to your downloads folder and double click 'Firefox Setup Stub.exe'

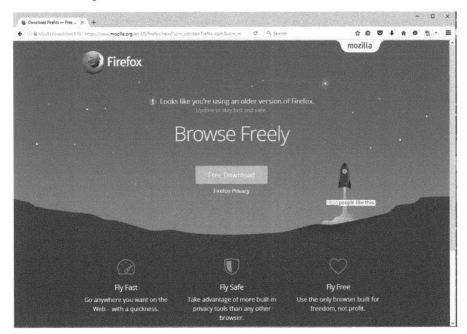

Follow the on screen instructions to install the browser.

Mail App

You can start the Mail App by tapping or clicking on the mail icon on your start menu.

If this is the first time you are using this app, you may be asked to add your email account.

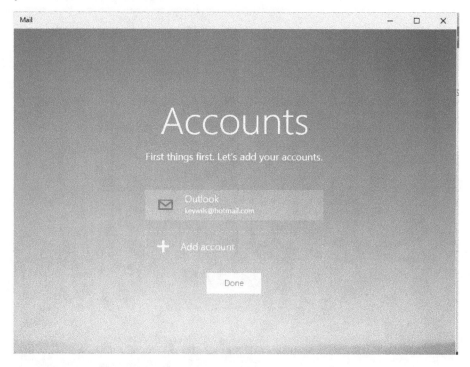

If you are using your Microsoft Account, mail app usually finds it as shown above.

Select this email account and click done.

Adding Other Email Accounts

If you have another email account such as Gmail or Yahoo you can add these too.

To do this click the settings icon on the bottom left of the screen.

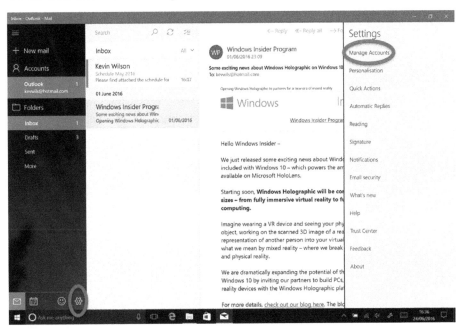

Click 'manage accounts', then 'add account' and enter the email username and password given to you by the account provider (Google, Yahoo, Apple, etc).

If your provider isn't in the list above click 'other account'.

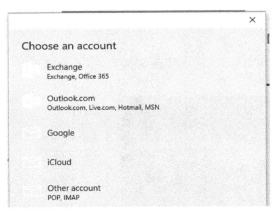

In this example, I want to add a Gmail account. So click on Google and in the dialog box that appears, enter your Gmail address and password.

Scroll down and click 'accept' at the bottom of the confirmation dialogue box.

All your email accounts will appear under the accounts section on the left hand side of the screen.

Using Mail

When you open mail app it will check for email, any new messages will appear in your inbox.

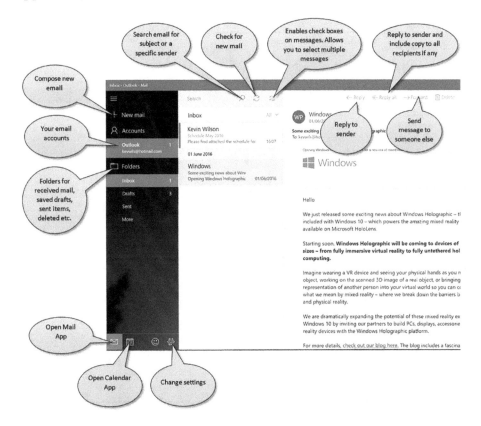

You can open any mail message by clicking on it, in your inbox. If you want to delete the message, swipe right to left across the message in your inbox. Or right click, select delete, if you are using a desktop computer.

To reply to the message, click the reply icon, at the top of the screen.

You'll see a screen that looks a bit like a word processor. Here you can type in your message. You can use the basic formatting tools such as bold text; click bold icon, and heading styles; click heading 1.

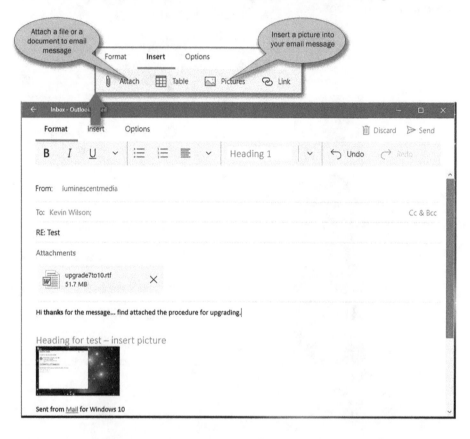

To attach a file, click 'insert' then select 'attach'. Select the file you want to attach.

Similarly if you want to insert an image, as shown above, click 'insert', then click 'pictures'. Select the photograph you want to insert.

Once you are done, click 'send'.

Calendar App

The calendar app links in with the mail app, you can find it on your start menu. It will either have a calendar icon or it will be displaying the current date.

If this is the first time you are using this app, you may be asked to add your email account.

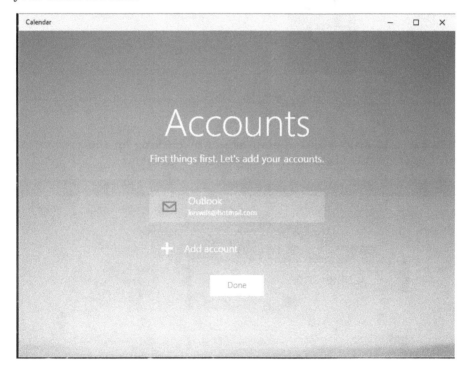

If you are using a Microsoft account, calendar app usually finds it for you. If this is the case select the account and click done.

If you use another email account click add account and enter your username/email and password details given to you by the account provider.

Once you have done that, you will see your main screen.

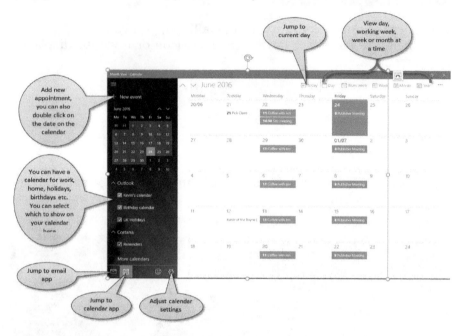

You can add events and appointments by clicking on the 'new event' button or double clicking on the date in the calendar.

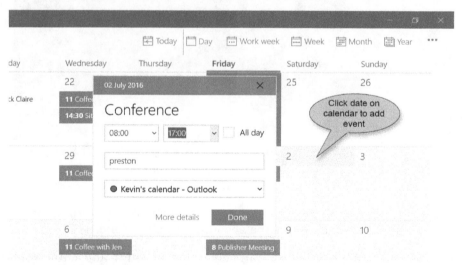

Type the location where you are meeting. Un-tick 'all day' and enter start and estimated finishing times. Unless it's an all day event.

Hit 'more details'.

You can add notes and any details about the event in the large text box at the bottom of the screen.

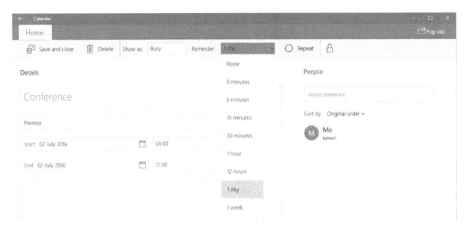

You can add a reminder too, by changing the reminder field. You can set it from none, 5 mins before, 15 mins before, a day before and so on. Reminders will pop up in your action centre as they occur.

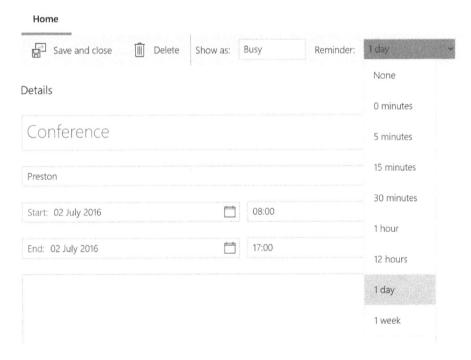

If the event is recurring, eg happens once a week or once a month, you can set this by clicking 'repeat'.

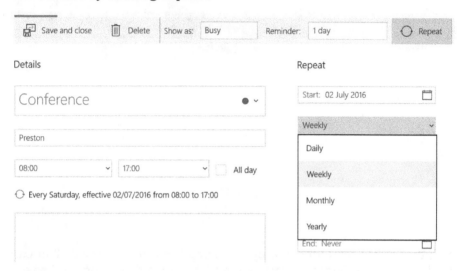

Under the 'repeat' section, you can set the event to occur on a daily, weekly, monthly and yearly basis. This saves you having to enter it for every occurrence. Also underneath, change any specifics such as days.

In the next bit, you can set the date your recurring event ends. Eg if it is a course it might be weekly for 6 months or a year.

Hit 'save and close' when you're done.

My People

The My People app brings communication to the forefront of Windows 10. You can pin the people you communicate with the most directly to your task bar. You can find the people app on your start menu

When the people app opens up, you'll see a list of your contacts.

To pin a contact to your task bar, right click on the contact's name and select 'pin to taskbar' from the popup menu. Select 'pin' from the conformation box that appears.

You'll see the person's profile picture appear on the bottom right of your taskbar. Click on the profile picture to open up their window.

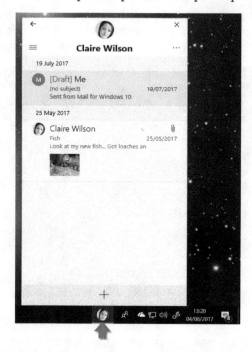

You can also drag files to the person's icon on the task bar if you want to share with them. If I wanted to share this file with Claire, I can drag and drop the file from file explorer onto her icon on the taskbar. The People App will open a contact window using your default method of contact - in this example, email. Add a message if you wish, then click 'send' to send the message.

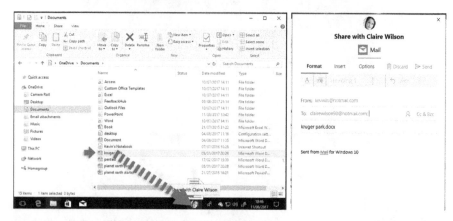

You'll also see notifications and incoming messages from these people.

FaceBook App

Go to the App Store and type 'facebook' into the search field on the right hand side of the screen.

Tap the 'facebook' icon that appears. Tap 'Free' or 'Install'.

Once the App installs, you can find it on your start menu, under 'recently added' at the top.

When you open the app, sign in with your facebook username and password. I'm not going through how to use facebook in this guide, but here you can use facebook as an app rather than through the website.

The app runs faster and you can post and share as you would normally with the website version.

Using the app version of facebook makes sharing on other apps easier, for example, sharing and posting photos from the photos app.

Skype

Microsoft has now integrated Skype into Windows 10. You can use it along with your Microsoft Account and your mobile/cell phone number.

You can access it by double clicking on the icon on your start menu. If you can't find it, type 'skype' into the search bar on the task bar.

Making a Call

You can either select someone's name from your call history, or select Phonebook or the People App, click on the contact's name and on their profile click 'Video Call' to place a Skype call.

The video call option will only appear on their profile if they are able to receive video calls.

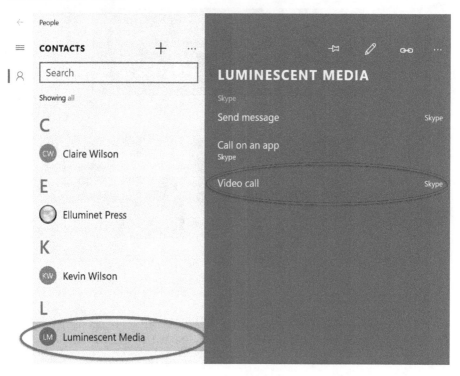

Once you click on Video Call, skype will open and attempt to connect to that person's skype account.

When the call comes through, the other person will get an alert on the bottom right of their screen. They can either accept or decline the call.

In the demo below, the tablet is calling the user logged on to the laptop, you can see the call screen on the tablet and the incoming call alert on the laptop.

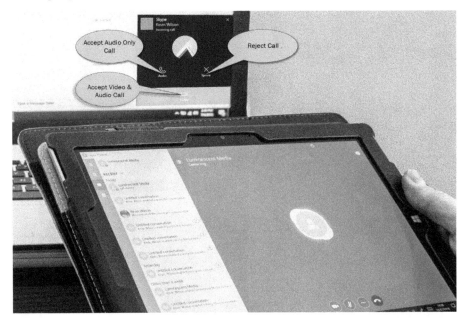

Once the other user picks up the call, you'll see an image of them on your screen.

You will also see a thumbnail view of yourself on the bottom right of the screen.

Along the bottom of the 'in call' screen you have 4 icons.

From left to right you have:

- Enable/disable web cam,
- Mute/un-mute microphone,
- Extra options (share your screen with another user, add another person to current call & speaker phone)
- End call.

In the demo below, Claire logged onto the tablet and placed a skype call to the user logged onto the laptop.

You can see on the laptop screen, the person you're talking to will appear in the large section of the window.

You will see a thumbnail view of yourself in the bottom right hand corner.

Screen Sharing

Another cool feature of Skype is the ability to share your desktop with the user you are having a skype call with.

This is a great way to keep in touch with people you don't see very often, as well as friends and family. It makes a great collaboration tool for business users too and enables you to share your screen to show photos, word documents, presentations etc.

In the demo below, the tablet on the right, is sharing its screen with the user logged onto the laptop. The tablet user is then able to launch any app, in this example, photos. Then the tablet user can open photos to show the other user.

The user on the laptop can see everything the tablet user is displaying on their screen.

Both users can still talk and see one another as if they were still in conversation. You'll see a thumbnail view of them in the bottom right hand corner of your screen.

To share your screen, make your video call as normal, then from the in call screen, tap the icon with the three dots.

From the menu that appears, click 'share screen'.

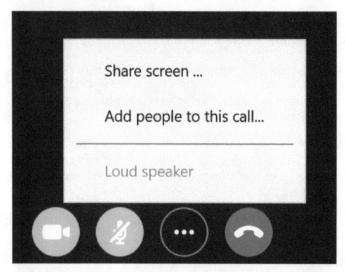

The other user will now be able to see everything on your screen.

Mobile Hotspot

Also known as tethering, this feature allows you to share your internet connection with your other devices and does this by creating a temporary WiFi hotspot. This can be useful if you have a 4G data connection on your phone but no WiFi available and need to access the internet on a tablet or laptop.

To enable your Wi-Fi hotspot, on your Windows Phone go to...

Settings App -> Network & Internet -> Mobile Hotspot

Flick the slider over to 'on'. Make a note of the network name and network password underneath.

On your laptop or tablet, tap on the WiFi icon on the right hand side of your taskbar. Windows 10 will scan for available WiFi networks. The network name you noted on your phone should appear. Tap on this network then tap 'connect'. Enter the password you noted on your phone and click 'next'.

Getting Things Done

To get things done on your laptop, you need apps or applications. You can download most apps from the Microsoft App Store. Others you may need to download from the manufacturer's website.

You need apps to edit your photos, listen to music, watch TV or a film, edit documents, create spreadsheets or databases and presentations.

Lets take a look at apps in the App Store.

App Store

You can purchase and download a wide variety of Apps for productivity, games, as well as film and television programs directly from the App Store.

You can find the app store by tapping on the icon on your start menu

Once the store opens you'll come to the main screen. Here you can search for apps by typing in the name in the search field. Or you can browse through the different categories.

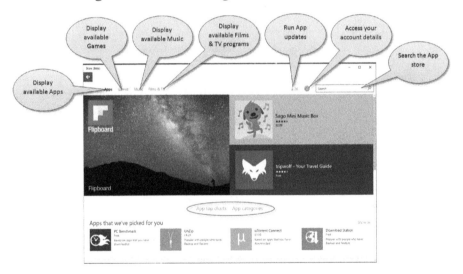

Some Apps and games you will need to pay for so you'll need to add payment details and others Apps and games are free.

If you click 'Apps' you will see a list of popular or trending apps.

Click 'App categories', circled above, and you will see a list of apps broken down in to categories such as kids and family for children's apps and things for them to do, productivity for apps such as office.

You can also search for specific types of apps by using the search field on the top right of the screen.

To buy an app, click on the App's icon to show a summary of what the app is and what it does.

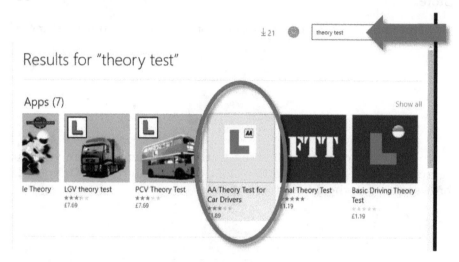

Click the price tag, circled above to purchase and download the app. You may need to enter your Microsoft Account email address and password.

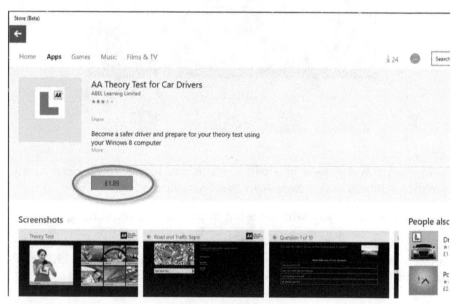

Once the app has downloaded and installed, you will be able to start your app using the start menu.

Maps App

You can find the maps icon on your start menu.

The maps app is useful for exploring parts of the world, landmarks and famous places. It is also useful for finding driving directions to different locations.

You can search for pretty much any address, country, place or landmark by typing it into the search field.

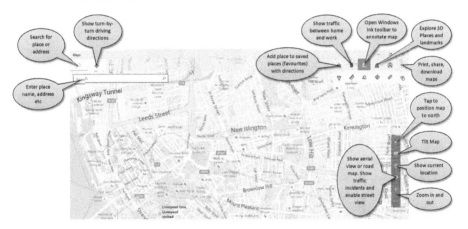

Maps App has an aerial map, and a road map. You can enable traffic flow, incident reporting, speed camera locations and street level view. To do this, select the 'map views' icon on the vertical bar on the right hand side to reveal the popup menu.

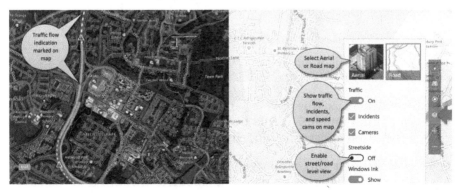

Get Directions

You can get driving directions to any location or address you can think of. You can get directions from your current location or you can enter a start location and a destination.

As well as driving directions you can get local bus routes and in some places even walking directions.

To get your driving directions, click or tap the turn-by-turn driving directions icon on the top left of your screen, labelled below.

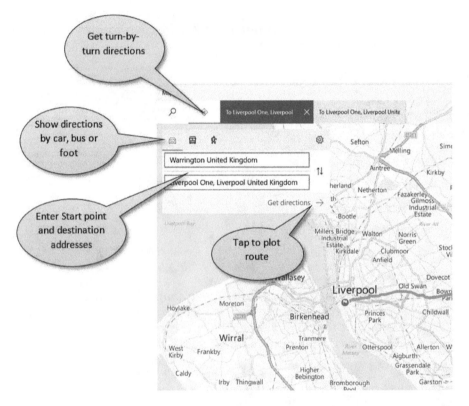

The first field will show your current location (Warrington in this example). You can also type in a location if you need to.

The second field is where you can enter your destination. Liverpool One Shopping Complex in this example. This can be a post code/zip code, residential address, town/city or place name.

Once you hit 'get directions' or tap the right arrow (next to your destination field), the maps app will calculate a route and display it on a map.

You'll see a map on the right hand side with a list of driving directions listed down the left hand side. You might see a choice of different routes, the quickest one is usually at the top.

You can click on any of these directions and the map will zoom in and show you the road on the map.

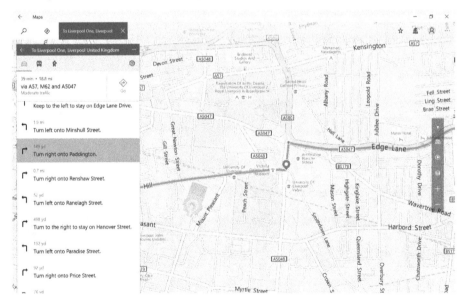

There is also an option to print the directions if needed but if you are using the maps app on your phone or tablet you can use it as a GPS or SatNav and the maps app will direct you as you drive.

Street View

Tap the maps view icon on the vertical bar on the right hand side. From the popup menu turn on 'streetside'. You'll notice some of the roads will be highlighted. Main roads and highways are in blue, minor roads are in light green. To go into street view, tap on the part of the road you want to see.

You'll see a street view of that section. To move forward, tap on a part of the road. To "look" left and right tap and drag your view to the left or right.

You can tap the part of the road you want to view on the map in the bottom pane.

Ink Directions

If I wanted to find some quick directions from my location or a specific location, to somewhere close by, I can draw directly onto the map and the Maps App will calculate a route. So in this example, I want to get from Westfield Primary School to Birch Road. Tap the Windows Ink icon, then select the directions icon from the drop down. Draw a line between your start and end points.

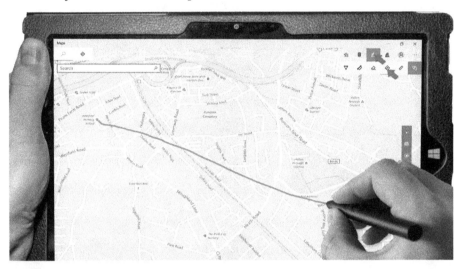

The Maps App will calculate the quickest route between your start and end points.

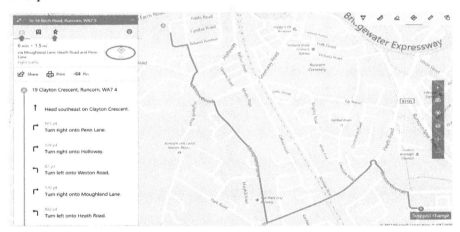

Down the left hand side, you'll see your turn-by-turn directions. Tap, the car icon for driving directions or tap, the little man icon for walking directions. Tap 'go' to start the navigation.

Measure Distances

Using the Windows Ink features, you can also measure distances between two points on the map.

Tap the Windows Ink icon, top right. Then from the drop down, select the measure tool.

Now with your pen, draw a line between the two points on the map, you want to measure.

Remember this tool doesn't take into account roads or paths on your map, just the relative length of the line you have drawn in relation to the scale of the map.

Annotations

Using the Windows Ink features, you can draw directly onto the map with your finger or pen.

Tap the Windows Ink icon, top right. Then from the drop down, select the ball-point pen tool.

From the drop down menu, select a colour from the palette and adjust the size using the slider underneath. Drag the bar to the right to increase the thickness

Now with your pen, draw directly onto the map.

You can share these annotations with friends/colleagues or print them out.

Chapter 5: Getting Things Done

Explore in 3D

This feature can come in hand if you want to explore landmarks or areas of interest.

You can have a look by clicking or tapping on the 'explore map in 3D' icon, circled below, and scrolling through the list down the left hand side of the screen.

Not all cities will be in 3D but the ones that are will appear in this list.

Down the left hand side you will see a number of famous landmarks and areas you can explore in 3D.

Perhaps you are going on holiday/vacation and you want to explore certain parts of the world you haven't been to - just remember the images you see aren't live and can be out of date.

Here you can see a fly-over view of a landmark. You can zoom in and out, rotate the map and move around as you explore.

Try also searching for your favourite place by typing it into the search field.

Weather App

The weather app can give you a forecast for your current location or any location you choose to view.

You can find the Weather app on your start menu. It is usually disguised as a live tile showing you weather summary for your current location.

When you first start weather app it will ask for your location, unless you have location services enabled, then it will automatically find your location.

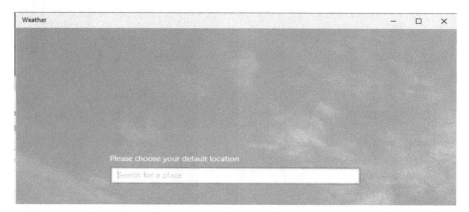

Once you have entered your location the weather app will show you a summary of the local weather conditions.

You can tap on each day to see more details, you may need to scroll down the page to see them.

Down the left hand side you have your navigation icons where you can see local weather, animated radar weather maps, historical weather and view your favourite locations list.

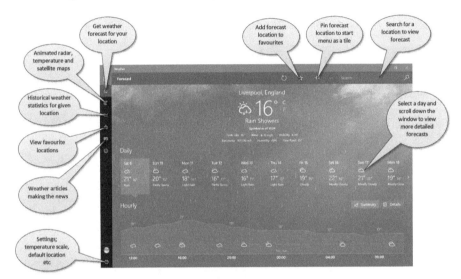

You can also find weather forecasts for other places. If for example you are going on holiday/vacation, you can enter the location's name into the search field and get a weather forecast.

You can also add forecasts for locations to your favourites list so you don't have to keep searching for them. To do this, just tap the 'add forecast location to favourites' icon along the top of your screen.

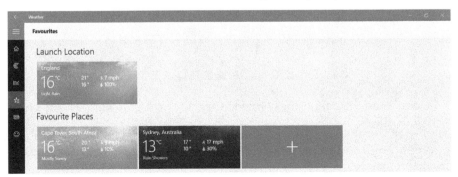

News App

You can find the news app icon on your start menu. It is usually a live tile and has up to date news headlines and images on the tile instead of an icon

The news app brings you local news headlines and stories from around the world.

Down the left hand side you have your navigation icons where you can browse different news sources such as news or sports channels.

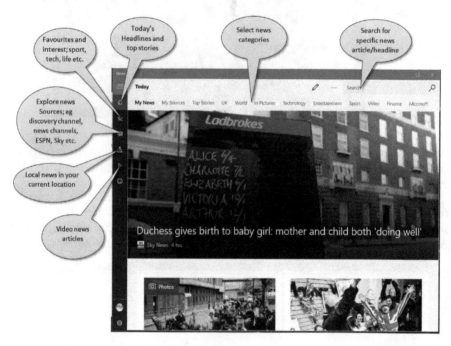

You can read the headlines, or local news, you can also watch video articles and reports.

You can find trending topics and news stories. Tap on the headlines to read the articles.

Alarms & Clock App

You can set alarms on your device, pc or phone to alert you. For example, setting a time to get up in the morning.

To do this tap the alarm tab, then tap the plus sign at the bottom of the window and enter the time.

Similarly if you wanted to add a clock for another city in the world, tap 'world clock', then tap the plus sign and enter the city/country name in the search field.

Chapter 5: Getting Things Done

This can be useful if you have colleagues or family in other countries, or just want to know what time it is there so when you skype them you aren't disturbing them in the middle of the night.

You can also create countdown timers, for example, to boil an egg for 3 minutes, time an exam for 50 minutes and so on.

Just tap timer, then tap the plus sign and enter the length of time.

Hit the play button to start the countdown.

Tap stopwatch to time something, for example, a race, lap times and so on.

Hit the play button to start the clock. Hit the flag icon to mark a lap.

Voice Recorder

Voice recorder is your on-board dictation machine. You can make voice notes, record lectures, interviews and so on. To start recording just hit the microphone icon on the screen.

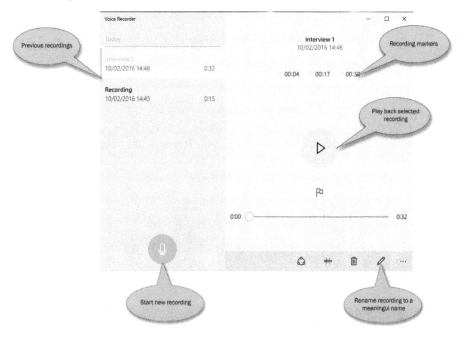

You can even add markers at important points during a recording.

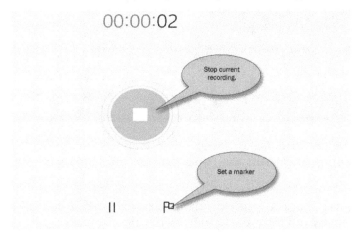

This way when you play back the recordings, you can go directly to the important points by clicking on these recording markers, illustrated in the top diagram.

157

eBooks

eBooks are now available through the App Store and can be purchased and downloaded directly to your device.

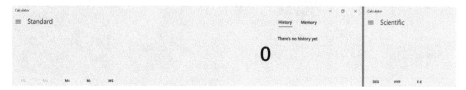

You'll see a new category called 'books', listed along the top left of the screen.

When you select the books category, you'll see a list of available books.

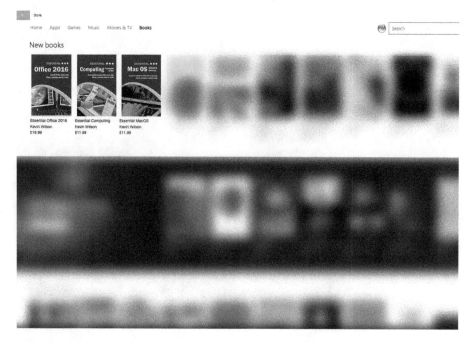

Here you'll see best sellers and recommended books from a variety of different genres. You can also browse for books in the different categories.

You can use the search field on the top right hand side of the store window, to search for a particular book title or author.

Once you have found the book you want, click the book cover.

You'll see a screen with the book's details; description, price, reviews and device compatibility.

Essential Office 2016

2016 · K. Wilson · Computers & The Internet

★★★★★ 1

£11.99

Description

Whether you're upgrading from a previous version or using it for the very first time, this book will guide you through Microsoft Office 2016 one step at a time, to help you understand the software more quickly and easily!

Techniques are illustrated systematically using photography and screen prints throughout, together with clear, concise and easy to follow text from an established expert in the field.

Whether you are new to Microsoft Office 2016, upgrading, or an experienced user needing an update, this book will provide you with a firm grasp of the underpinning foundations, and equip you with the skills needed to use Microsoft Office 2016 effectively and productively.

More

Available on

PC   Mobile

Capabilities

Text to speech
Read on up to 6 devices

Click 'buy' to purchase the book. You'll need your Microsoft Account email address and password. You may also be prompted for a payment method if you haven't added one to your Microsoft Account.

Your books will appear in Microsoft Edge Book Library.

Reading eBooks

You can now read your purchased eBooks in Microsoft Edge. To see your purchased books, click the 'hub' icon, circled below-top. Next, click the 'book shelf' icon, indicated with the red arrow below.

All the books you have purchased from the store will appear here, click on the cover to open the book.

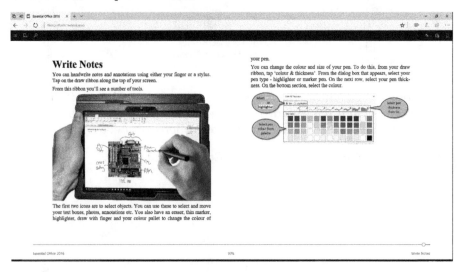

Calculator App

The calculator app works like any calculator. You'll find it on your start menu

You can choose the type of calculator you want; just a standard calculator for adding a few numbers together or a full scientific calculator for working out more complex equations. To change the calculator click the icon on the top left of your screen, and select 'scientific'.

Unit Converter

You can also convert different units. You can convert between different currencies, weight, length, temperature, energy and so on. To open the converter, click the icon on the top left of your screen, shown below.

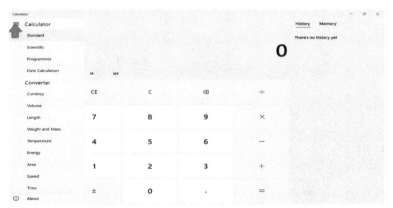

Useful if you're away somewhere and want to convert the local currency to your own. Or convert metric measurements to ones you're familiar with.

Currency Converter

Click the icon on the top left of your screen and select 'currency' from the drop down menu.

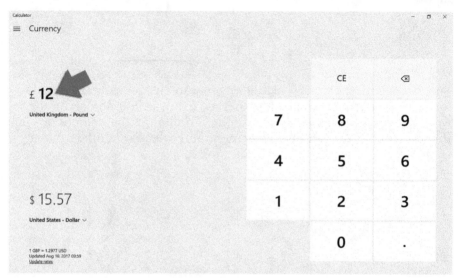

Tap on the currency numbers and enter a value using the on screen keypad, as shown above.

To change the currencies, click the currency name under the value, shown below. From the popup menu, select the currency you want. In the example below, I'm converting from British Pounds to US Dollars.

Photos App

The photos app is a nice little way to organise your photos and works whether you are on a tablet, phone or desktop PC.

You can find the photos app on the start menu.

Photos app will import photos directly from your digital camera or on-board camera if you are using a tablet or phone.

You can also perform minor corrections and enhancements such as removing red-eye, lightening up a dark photograph or apply some simple effects such as sepia or black and white.

To do this, tap or click on an image, this will open the image in view mode.

Chapter 5: Getting Things Done

This will give you some options to share a photograph via email or social media, see the image full screen, edit it or delete it. You can tap the magic wand icon to perform some automatic adjustments such as brightness, contrast etc.

You can also tap the pencil icon to do your own editing and photo enhancements.

If you tap or click the pencil icon you will enter edit mode. In edit mode, you will see a panel open up on the right hand side. At the top of the panel you can tap 'crop and rotate' to crop your photo or rotate it. Underneath you have two categories of options. The first is enhance, and allows you to apply filters and effects to your photos. The second is adjust, and allows you to adjust the brightness, contrast, shadows, highlights and colour correction to your photos.

If I wanted to crop my zebra photo, I could do so using the crop icon at the top of the side panel. You'll notice a box appear around the photo. Click and drag the white circles to resize the box so it surrounds the part of the photo you want to keep, as shown below.

Tap 'done' when you're happy. You can also rotate your image to get it level. Drag the control handle, circled below, to line up the horizon with the lines on the grid, or any vertical or horizontal lines to level up the photo.

Tap 'done', when you're happy.

Also if you wanted to adjust the brightness, select the 'adjust' tab on the right hand panel, tap 'light', and all your lighting adjust tools will appear underneath (contrast, exposure, shadows and highlights), as shown in the illustration below.

Use the sliders underneath to adjust the levels.

Hit 'save' when you're done to save the adjustments you have made. The procedure is the same for all other adjustments, effects and fixes.

You can also post or share your favourites to facebook or email, just tap 'share'. In the example below, I posted this one on facebook.

Tap the back arrow on the top left of the screen to get back to your collections.

You can also draw on your photographs too using the 'draw icon' on the edit screen.

Draw with your pen or finger to annotate your photograph.

Along the top of your screen you'll see a tool bar. You can select from three different writing tools. A pen, a pencil which gives you a nice pencil look to your drawings, and a calligraphy pen.

The next icon along is an eraser, this allows you to use your pen or finger to run out parts of your drawing.

The next icon along toggles between writing with your finger and writing with your pen stylus.

You can also save and share the photos with your annotations using the share and save icons.

Story Remix

A new feature called 'story remix', originally a stand alone app but now integrated into the Photos App, allows you to quickly and easily blend mixed reality, 3D, photos and videos into a video clip that you can share on social media or use to promote an idea or business.

Creating Remixes

To create a remix video, click 'collection' then click 'create'. From the drop down menu, select 'video remix'.

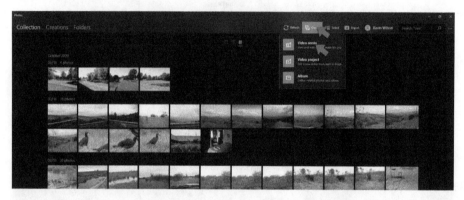

Click the photos/videos you want to include in your remix.

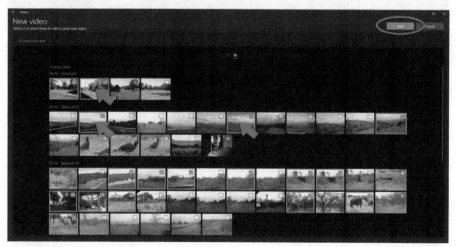

Click 'add', when you're done.

The Photos App will mix the video and photos, add a theme and some music.

When it's finished, you'll be able to see a preview of the video remix has created. Hit 'remix it for me' to have the Photos App remix another video. If you're happy with it, the remix will be saved to your creations section and you can share to social media or export as a video file.

Sharing Remixes

If you haven't already opened your remix, go to the creations section and select a remix you want to share.

To share it click, 'export and share'. Select 'best for online sharing'

Select 'share on social media, email or another app', then select your social media app, eg, facebook.

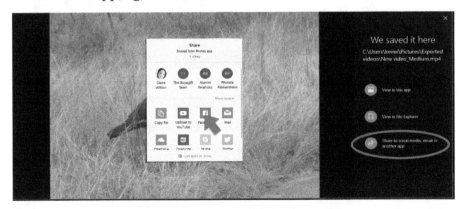

Editing & Customising Remixes

If you want to make some customisations to your video, perhaps change the music, order of photographs or add some text, click 'edit video' if prompted.

You'll see the main editing screen. Lets take a look at the different parts.

Along the bottom, you'll see the order of photos/videos you have added. To reorder these, drag them across to the position in the sequence you want them.

170

Add Text Titles

You can add text to your video. First, select the photo you want the text to appear. In this example, I am going to add a title, so I'm going to select the first photo. Select a template from the bottom right (I'm going to choose 'electric'), type your title into the text field on the top right.

Select where you want the text to appear: centre, top, left; using the 'choose layout' section on the bottom right. Click 'done' on the top right when you're finished.

Add Music

Now, how about some music. Since this is a remix of our Safari trip, I'm going to use the 'road trip' music - seems appropriate. So select the music option on the top right of the screen, from the popup window select 'explorer'.

Chapter 5: Getting Things Done

You can also add your own music if you prefer. Click on 'your music' then 'select a music file'.

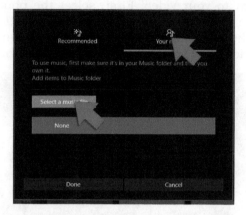

Navigate to your music folder on your computer - this is usually called 'music' and select a track.

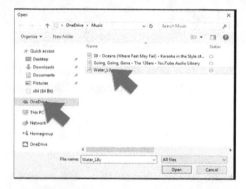

Select the track in the preview screen. Click 'done' when your happy.

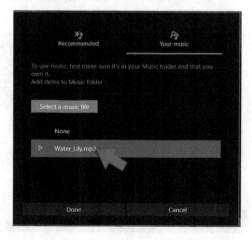

Slideshow Motion

To change the motion of your photographs in your slideshow, select the photo slide you want to change.

Now select a motion style from the options on the right hand side of the screen

Here you can select 'zoom in right', which will slow zoom into the right hand side of the image; or 'zoom in left' zooms into the left hand side of the image. These are useful if the subject in the photograph is on the left or right hand side of the image - helps draw attention to your subject. You can also pan across the image or zoom into the centre.

Export & Share your Creations

You can share your creations via email or post on social media. To do this click 'export or share' on the top right of your screen.

From the popup dialog box, select the quality of your video. If you are sending the video to someone over email, select small as email doesn't support large file sizes - this is also the lowest quality.

More often than not, you'll want to share your work on social media. For this, select medium - this is better quality.

If you intend to watch on your computer click large. This is the best quality

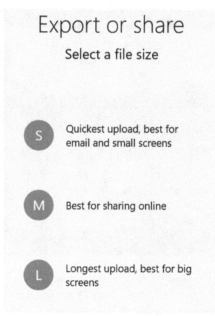

For this example, I am going to select medium (M).

Now, to share it on social media, click 'share to social media, email or another app', on the bottom right.

From the popup menu, select a contact from the top of the list so send using 'my people' or select your favourite social media app in the section at the bottom of the popup.

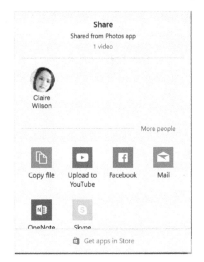

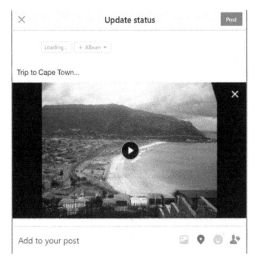

In this example, I am posting to facebook. Click 'facebook', your creation will appear in a post ready for you to add a caption.

Groove Music App

You can find the music app icon on your start menu

When you start Groove Music for the first time, it will automatically scan your computer for music and add it to your library. Click 'lets go' once the "setting things up" scan is complete.

You'll land on Groove Music's main screen. From here you can play your music, buy music from the store, or stream it to your device if you have a Music Pass. Let's take a look at the main screen.

To reveal the menu, tap the hamburger icon on the top left. ≡

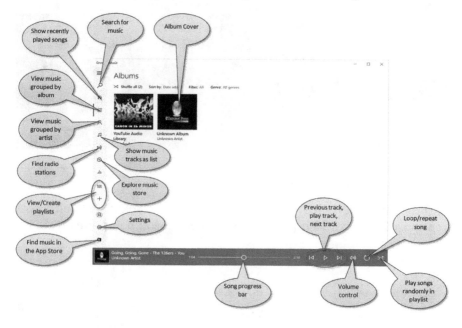

To view albums

Here you can see all the songs on this machine listed in order they were added. You can also sort them by artist and album by clicking on the links down the left hand side of the screen.

You can also buy music by clicking on the 'get music in store' link on the bottom left of the screen.

You can tap/click on a track to purchase and download it. If you are looking for a specific artist or track name, you can type it into the search field on the top right of the screen.

Groove Music Pass

A Groove Music Pass gives you access to the whole music store for a monthly subscription fee. With this pass you can stream millions of tracks directly to your device.

To apply for a pass, click the settings icon on the bottom left of the Groove Music window.

At the top of the screen tap 'get a groove music pass'

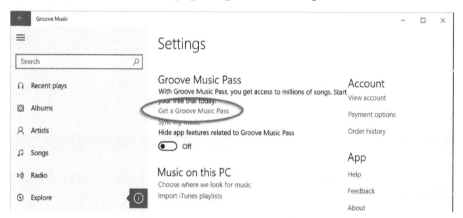

Hit subscribe on the next window, and enter your Microsoft Account username and password. You will also need some kind of payment details. Follow the instructions on the screen to enter payment details if haven't already done so.

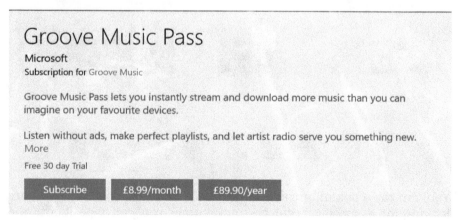

Remember you can get a 30 day trial, after that you can either pay the subscription and continue using the service, or cancel your subscription.

You can now search for any of your favourite bands, artists and albums and stream them directly to your device. Just type the names into the search field at the top of your screen.

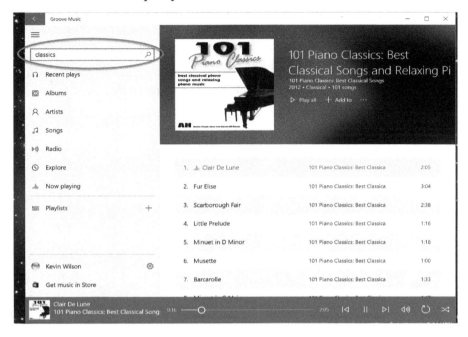

You can add your favourites to playlists by right clicking on the track and selecting 'add to'. From the slide out menu click on a playlist, or tap 'new playlist' to create a new one.

All your playlists will appear on the left hand side of your screen.

Game Mode

Game mode is designed to enhance the performance of games on Windows 10 by giving processing priority to the game. This means that more resources such as CPU and GPU processing time is given to the game, as well as more RAM and reducing the resources used by background processes and apps.

If you go to the Settings App, you'll see a new category called 'gaming'.

On the left hand side click 'game mode'. Set the slider to 'on' to enable 'Game Mode'.

Film & TV App

You can find the Film & TV app on your start menu.

With the video app you can add and watch your own videos taking with your phone or camera and those downloaded from the internet.

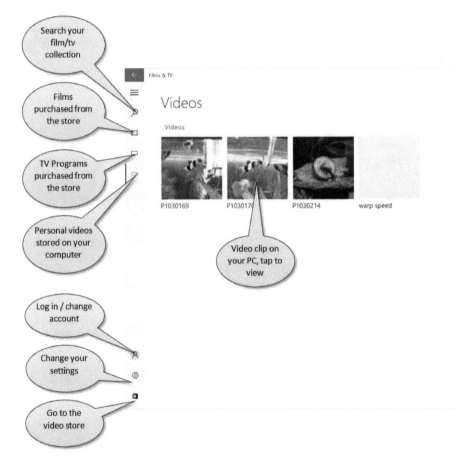

You can also purchase/rent films and television programs and watch them using this app.

To do this, tap the 'go to store' icon on the bottom left of the screen.

Chapter 5: Getting Things Done

You will need to sign in with your Microsoft Account to make any purchases. You will be prompted for your account info when you click on buy or rent.

Search for the name of the TV show or film using the search field on the top right of the screen.

In the results that show up, tap on the thumbnail of the one you want.

On the next screen, tap the rent or buy button.

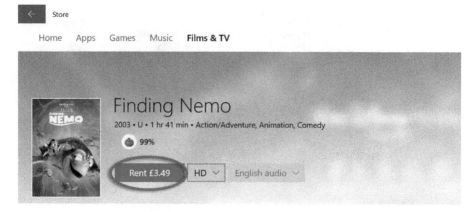

All your rented and purchased movies will appear in the films or TV sections shown below.

You can also view your own videos that you have taken with a digital camera or the camera on your phone. To access this, click on the 'personal videos' icon, on the left hand side of the screen.

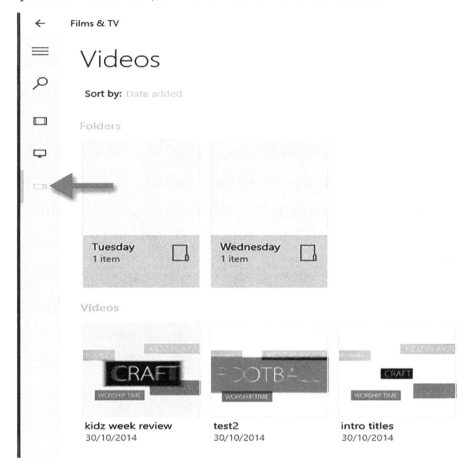

Here you can click on the thumbnails of your videos, as shown above, to view them. Click the back arrow, located in the top left corner, to get back to the main screen from your video.

Picture-in-Picture

Also known as 'compact overlay' and allows you to watch a small video window in the corner of your screen while working in another app. In the video window, you'll see a new icon, circle below. This icon will appear in the video window on most apps as well as youtube videos in the Edge browser.

Just click this icon and the video will shrink to the top right of the screen. You can them click and drag this window to any part of your screen. I find the bottom right is a good place to put it if you're working on something else.

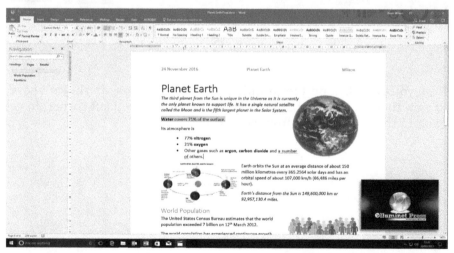

Playing DVDs

If you like watching DVDs on your PC, Windows 10 can't them out of the box, so you'll have to download a free player instead.

The best one I found is VLC media player, which can play DVDs, CDs and a range of other file types.

Just go to their website and download the software.

`www.videolan.org`

Click 'Download VLC', click 'Run' when prompted and follow the instructions on screen.

DVDs are becoming obsolete thanks to high speed internet services available to most homes and video/film streaming services that allow you to access on demand films and television programs right from the comfort of your arm chair.

Many computers, particularly laptops and mobile devices no longer include a DVD player. You can still buy external USB DVD drives if you need them.

Microsoft Office 365

Microsoft Office 365 is a subscription based service that gives you email as well as access to Microsoft Office: Word, Excel, PowerPoint, Publisher, etc. You'll need a Microsoft Account to access the software.

Create a Microsoft Account

To set up a Microsoft Account you'll need to open your web browser.

Go to the following website

```
signup.live.com
```

You will see a form asking for your details.

Enter all the required details in the fields then scroll down the form. Once you have filled in all the details click 'create account' at the bottom.

Enter the characters you see

☐ Send me promotional offers from Microsoft. You can unsubscribe at any time.

Clicking **Create account** means that you agree to the Microsoft Services Agreement and privacy and cookies statement.

Create account

Purchasing Office Online

Open your web browser and go to Microsoft office website

```
products.office.com
```

In this example we are purchasing the home premium version. If you want to download a different version change it by clicking 'office products' and selecting the version from the drop down box. The procedure is the same.

From the home page select 'For Home'

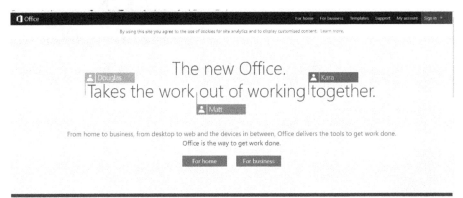

Click 'buy now' in the Office 365 Home column.

You can either pay a monthly subscription or pay an annual cost. Choose depending on your budget.

Paying monthly will spread the cost over the year rather than paying one lump sum.

Select 'buy now'. In this example I am going to pay monthly. Click 'review and checkout'

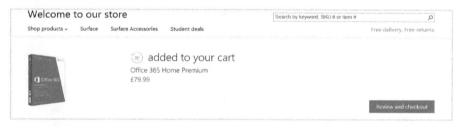

Click 'next' to confirm your order.

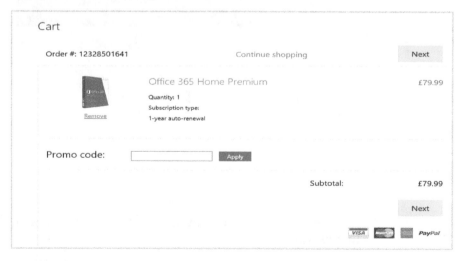

Once you have done that you will be prompted to sign in with your Microsoft account.

If you are using Windows 8 or 10 you will probably already have a Microsoft account that you created when you set up your machine.

This is usually the username/email and password you used to sign into Windows.

Enter these details into the screen below.

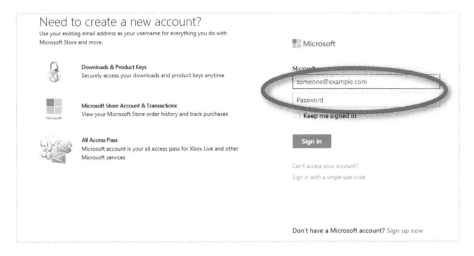

You will be prompted to enter your payment details. If you have purchased from the Microsoft store before then you can choose to pay with an existing card or you can add a different card number.

Enter your information in all the fields.

Click next at the bottom of the screen then review and confirm your order.

Cancel   Next

Microsoft is committed to helping protect your privacy. For more info, see our privacy and cookies.

Microsoft will send you a comfirmation email.

Downloading Office 2016 Suite

If Office doesn't update itself automatically, you can update your Office installation on your computer by navigating to the following website and login into your Office 365 account.

office.com

Sign in with your Microsoft Account details

Scroll down to the bottom of the page and click on 'My Account'

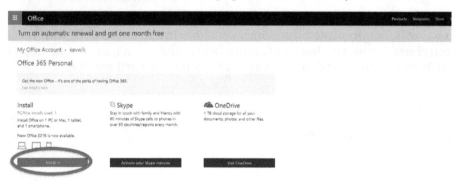

From 'My Office Account' page click 'install'

Click 'run' when prompted by your web browser

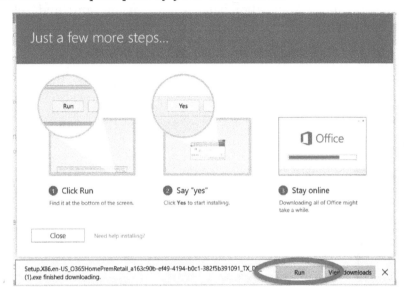

The Office installer will run and begin downloading the necessary files to install Office 2016 on your computer.

This can take a while to complete depending on the speed of your computer and your internet connection.

The Installer will run once it has finished downloading. You may need to enter your computer's password you used to log into Windows.

Once Office is installed, click 'close'

You're all set! Office is installed now
Click Start > All Apps.

Close

You will be able to find your Office 2016 Apps installed on your start menu. You may have to go to 'app apps' if you don't see any tiles or shortcuts on your start menu.

If this is not your computer and belongs to someone else in the family, open up an office application such as Microsoft word and select a blank document.

If this is your own computer then you can skip this step.

Click file from the top left hand side and from the screen that appears, shown below, select 'account'.

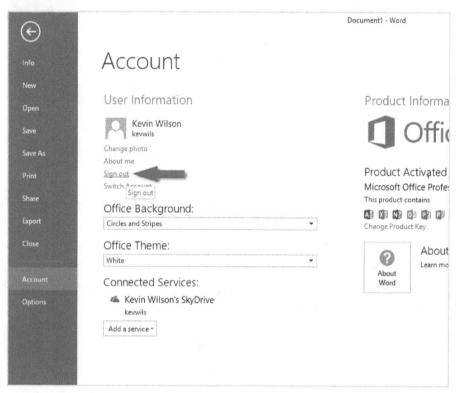

In the main window, Click on 'sign out'

This will allow that person to sign in using their own Microsoft account, rather than using yours.

Check out the book Essential Office 365 for more details on how to use Microsoft Office Applications.

Open Office

Open Office is a free alternative to Microsoft Office. It isn't quite as advanced or rich in features, but it's ideal for basic word processing, spreadsheets and presentations.

You can download the software from

`www.openoffice.org/download`

From the website, click 'download full installation'.

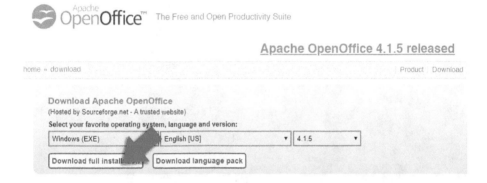

Once the download is complete, click on the download prompt at the bottom of your browser.

If it doesn't show up, go to your downloads folder and double click on the program, then follow the on-screen instructions.

`Apache_OpenOffice_4.1.5_Win_x86_install_en-US.exe`

Chapter 5: Getting Things Done

Once Open Office is installed, you'll find an icon on your desktop. Double click this icon to start the application.

Here you'll see the home screen. Select 'text document' to start typing letters or other documents. You can also create spreadsheets, presentations, basic drawings and create databases.

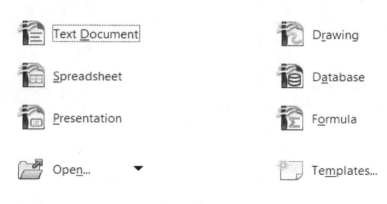

Google Drive

Google Drive allows you to store documents, photos and other media online. Google Drive also has a word processor called Google Docs, a spreadsheet program called Google Sheets, and a presentation program called Google Slides.

Create a Google Account

To use Google Docs, you'll need a Google Account or GMail Account. If you use Google Mail or GMail, then you probably already have one. To create a Google Account, go to...

`accounts.google.com/SignUp`

Fill in the form with your details...

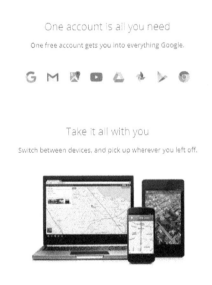

Click 'next step'.

Creating Documents, Spreadsheets & Presentations

Using your web browser go to the following website, and sign in with your Google Account.

`drive.google.com`

Select 'new'. Here you can create new documents.

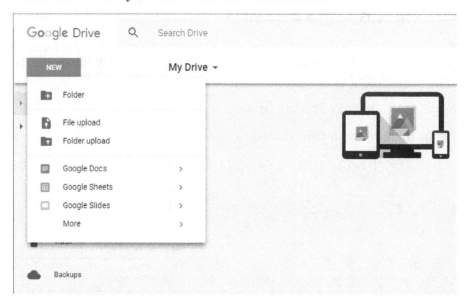

Click 'google docs'. This will create a new document for you to type.

You can also create spreadsheets, and presentation slides.

You'll also find your saved documents in your Google Drive

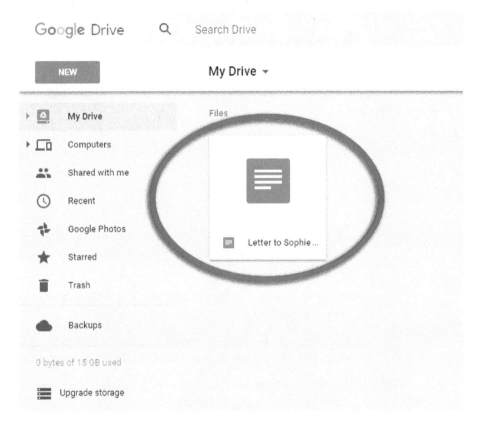

We'll go into more detail in Essential Chromebooks and Productivity Apps.

Chapter 6

Maintaining your Laptop

Laptop maintenance keeps your laptop in a good working order.

Using anti-virus software, backing up files, keeping your computer up to date.

Also more technical issues such as file de-fragmentation, disk clean-ups and start-up programs.

System backup and recovery procedures and advice when your PC has problems.

Here we will take a look at some common areas and procedures to keep your machine running smoothly

Anti-Virus Software

A lot of this software is sold pre-installed on the machine you buy and is offered on a subscription basis. So you have to pay to update the software.

There are some however that are available for free to home users.

Windows Defender

Windows 10 comes pre-installed with Windows Defender which is automatically updated by Microsoft for free.

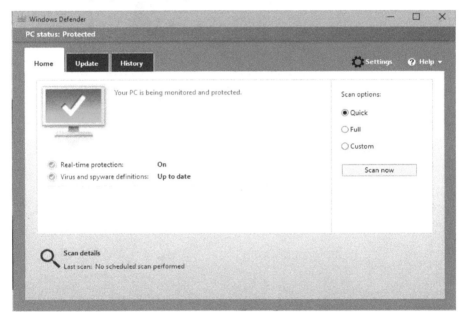

This is the bare essentials and is the minimum protection against viruses and online threats. This is adequate if you just browse the web and check your email. If you do online banking or shop online, then you should have a look at some of the more advanced security software packages.

Two free ones that are a good place to start are Avast and AVG. Both of these packages are very good. The free one is basic, but you can upgrade if you need something more.

Avast

Avast scans and detects vulnerabilities in your home network, checks for program updates, scans files as you open them, emails as they come in and fixes PC performance issues.

You can download it from their website.

www.avast.com

Scroll down the page until you find 'free download'.

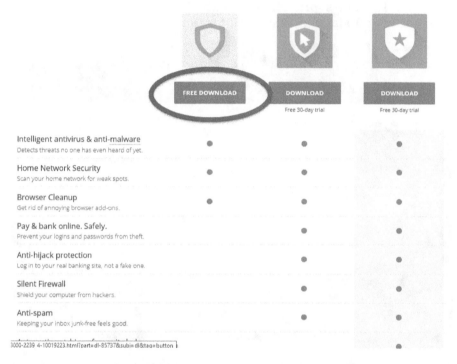

The other two versions here are 30 day trials and will expire after 30 days. You will need to pay a subscription to continue.

When prompted hit 'install'. If the installation doesn't run automatically, go to your downloads folder and run 'avast_free_antivirus_setup.exe', follow the on screen wizard.

AVG

AVG blocks viruses, spyware, & other malware, scans web, twitter, & facebook links and warns you of malicious attachments.

You can download it from their website.

www.avg.com

Compare Products   Features   System Requirements

Or choose what's best for you

	AntiVirus FREE 2015	AntiVirus 2015	Internet Security 2015
Antivirus Blocks viruses, spyware, & other malware	✓	✓	✓
Link Protection Scans web, Twitter®, & Facebook® links	✓	✓	✓
Email Protection Warns you of malicious attachments		✓	✓
Online Shield Protects you from harmful downloads		✓	✓
Data Safe Encrypts & password-protects private files		✓	✓
More Frequent Auto-Updates Get automatic security updates every 2 hours		✓	✓
Anti-Spam Keep your inbox free of spam & scams			✓
Shopping Protection Shop & bank safer with Enhanced Firewall			✓

Money-Back Guarantee
Buy without risk! If you're not satisfied in the first 30 days, we'll refund your money. Learn more

FREE Download	FREE Trial	FREE Trial
	Buy Now	Buy Now

The other two versions here are 30 day trials and will expire after 30 days. You will need to pay a subscription to continue.

Security Centre

Introduced in the Creator's Update, Windows Defender Security Centre is a hub for all your Windows security features including virus protection, device health, networking, firewalls, internet security, app control and family safety options.

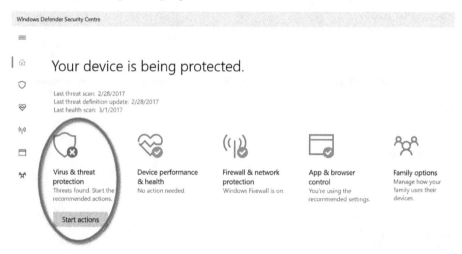

Virus & Threat Protection

From here you can launch Windows Defender or a 3rd party anti virus app. Security Centre will alert you of any potential threats, as shown above, and invite you to 'start actions' using your installed anti virus app or Windows Defender. Click 'start actions'.

From the summary page, click 'clean threats' to launch your anti virus app.

From your anti virus app, in this case Windows Defender, click 'clean pc', then from the popup, set the recommended action to 'remove' next to each detected threat, if not already done.

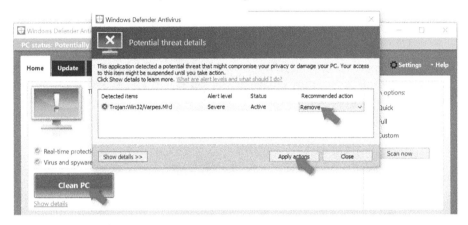

Then click 'apply actions'. This will clean your device.

Device Performance & Health

Here you can see any issues arising with drivers, updates, battery life and disk storage space. You also have the option to refresh Windows 10, meaning you can re-install Windows if it is not running smoothly while keeping your personal files safe.

Firewall & Network Protection

Here you can troubleshoot network issues with WiFi or internet connectivity and adjust your firewall settings

App & Browser Control

Here you can adjust your browser and application security settings such as SmartScreen filter that helps protect you against malicious websites, apps and downloads.

Family Options

This section links you to your family options using your web browser and allows you to monitor your kids' online activity.

Controlled Folder Access

This feature allows you to protect files & folders from modification by unapproved applications and malware. If any of these applications tries to modify files, you'll get a notification allowing you to block the action.

To enable this feature, open Windows Defender Security Center, Click 'Virus & threat protection settings', scroll down the page, then select 'Controlled folder access'.

Set the switch to 'On'.

Windows Defender will normally allow most known applications to access and change data in the folders on your machine. If Windows Defender detects an app it doesn't recognise, you'll receive a notification that it has been blocked. Some of the time this will be a legitimate application. To add other applications to the 'safe list', click 'allow an app trough controlled folder access'.

Click 'add an allowed app'.

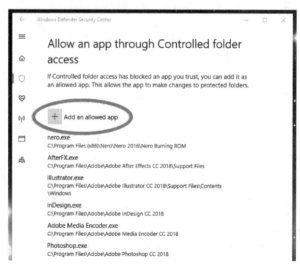

Now in the dialog box that appears, navigate to the folder where the application is installed. This will usually be "C:\Program Files". In this example, I'm going to add 'Adobe After Effects'. So navigate to the folder in 'program files'. Make sure you select the file with the EXE extension, as shown below.

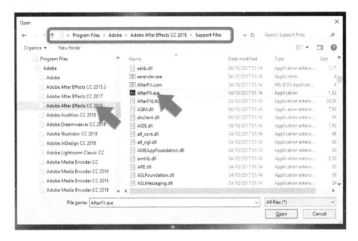

Windows Defender will automatically add your system folders and most of your personal folders. You can add any others if you need to. To do this, click 'protected folders' on the 'virus & threat protection' screen.

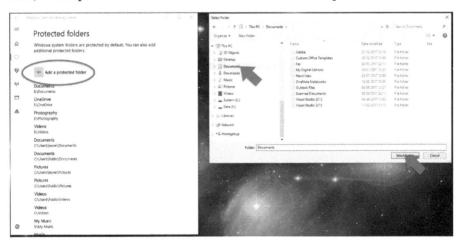

Click 'add a protected folder', then from the dialog box that appears, navigate to the folder you want to protect, click on it, then click 'select folder'.

Exploit Protection

This feature is designed to protect your PC from various types of exploits out of the box and shouldn't need any configuration.

To find this feature, open Windows Defender Security Center, click 'App & browser control' then select 'Exploit protection'.

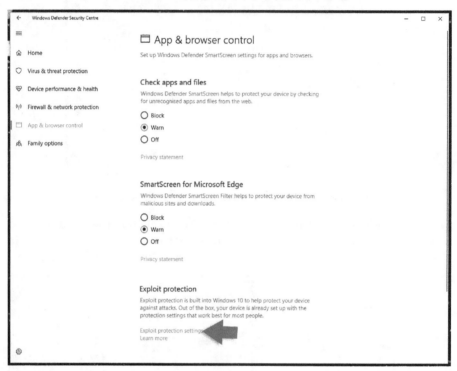

Backing Up your Files

If you have ever lost data because of a computer glitch or crash you know how frustrating it can be. So we all need a good backup strategy. I'm going to go through the strategy I have found that has worked well over the years.

Creating a Backup

First of all go buy yourself a good external hard disk. This is a small device that plugs into a USB port on your computer. Below is a typical specification for an external hard disk

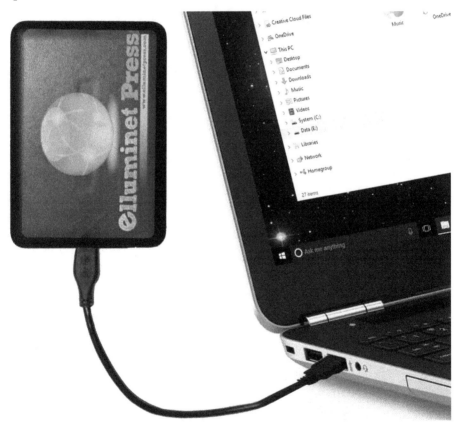

Plug in your external drive into a free USB port.

Chapter 6: Maintaining your Laptop

In the search field on the task bar type 'file history'.

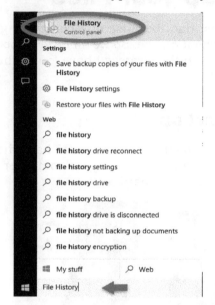

Click 'File History' in the search results, circled above.

On the screen that appears, click 'Turn On' to enable File History.

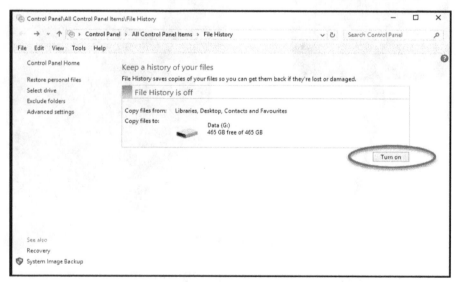

Once you have turned on File History, Windows 10 will start to copy files from your libraries (documents, pictures, music etc) onto your external hard drive.

Adding Folders

If you want to add folders to your backup, just add them to your libraries. Remember your desktop, documents, photos, music & videos folders and their contents are already included.

For example, if I wanted to include my photography folder which is on another hard drive, open file explorer, right click on the folder and go down to 'include in library'. Then from the slide-out menu, click 'create new library'.

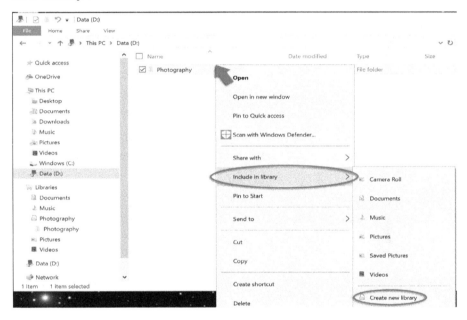

You'll see your libraries listed in the left hand pane.

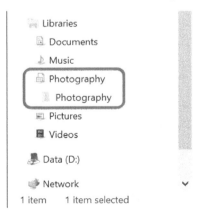

This folder will now be backed up with the rest of your libraries

Setting Backup Schedules

By default, File History saves files every hour, but you can change this by clicking on "Advanced Settings" listed down the left hand side of the screen.

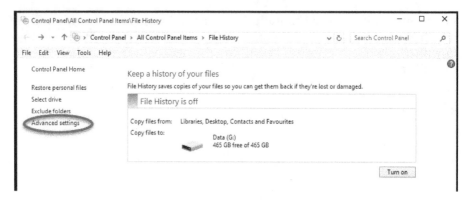

A good guide is to set how often File History saves files to "Daily". This will tell File History to save copies of your files once a day. For most users this is sufficient.

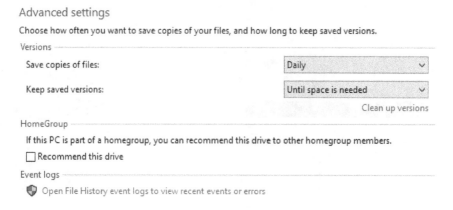

Set 'keep saved versions' to 'until space is needed'. This means that File History will keep creating backups while there is sufficient space on the hard drive, then once the drive fills up, File History will start to delete the oldest backups to make space for new backups.

Good practice would be to plug in your external drive at the end of each day to back up what you have done throughout the day.

Backups can take a while depending on how much you have done.

Restoring Files

Plug in your external Hard drive. Open up File History and click 'Restore Personal Files'

Use the left and right arrows at the bottom to navigate to the date backed up when you know your file still existed or was working.

Then in the library section double click in the folder the file was in eg pictures if you lost a photo.

Select the photo and to restore it click the green button at the bottom of the window.

Password Recovery

You can recover a forgotten Microsoft account password from the login screen. You'll see a "Reset password" or "I forgot my PIN" link below the password box.

Enter your Microsoft Account email address and the captcha characters, then click 'next'

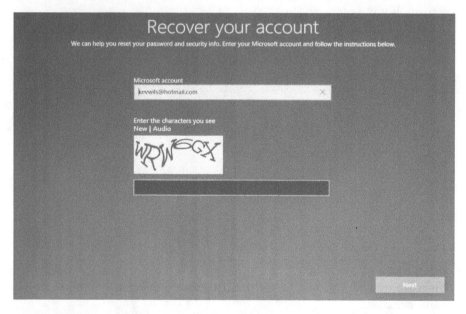

Here you'll see your recovery email address. This is the alternative email address you entered when you signed up for a Microsoft Account.

Select the address reminder then type the full address in the field below. Click 'send code'.

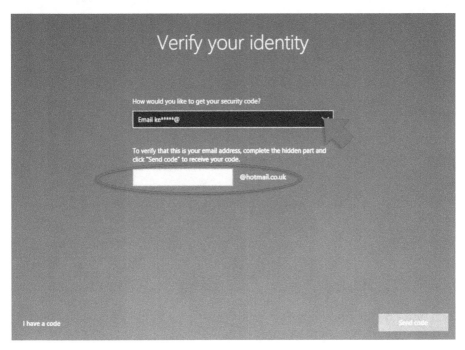

Now, log into the recovery email account and check your mail, you'll see an email with a code. Enter the code in the field below and click 'next'.

Enter your new password.

You will now be able to log on using your new password. Click 'next' to go back to the lock screen.

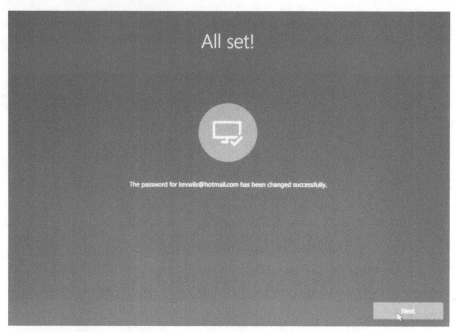

Windows Update

Windows update usually automatically downloads and installs all updates available for windows.

The Unified Update Platform or UUP allows targeted updates meaning Windows Update will only download the changes and updates included since the last update that are relevant to your version of Windows 10. This will mean smaller downloads and quicker updates.

Settings

You can find Windows Update in the Settings App on the start menu. Select 'update & recovery', then click 'windows update'.

Update & recovery
Windows Update, back-up, recovery

Lets take a look at some of the options

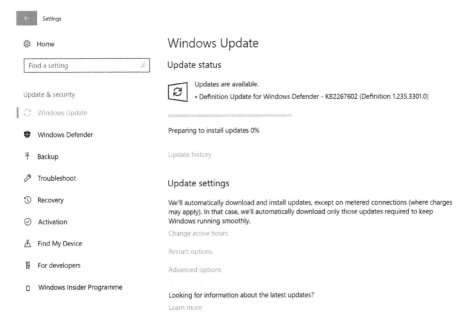

Scheduled Updates

Once Windows Update has downloaded the updates, it will schedule a system restart, if one is required to install the updates.

This is usually scheduled according to your specified 'active hours', which means Windows Update will not restart during these hours.

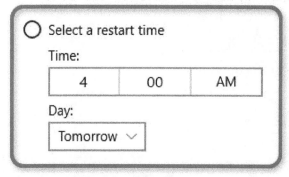

A restart has been scheduled

If you want, you can restart now. Or, you can reschedule the restart to a more convenient time. Be sure your device is plugged in at the scheduled time. The install may take 10-20 minutes.

⦿ We'll schedule a restart during a time you usually don't use your device (right now 4:00 tomorrow looks good).

◯ Select a restart time

Time:

| 4 | 00 | AM |

Day:

Tomorrow ⌄

Bandwidth Limiting

Constant updates can eat up your internet bandwidth leaving very little for you to browse the web, skype and do your work.

With this in mind, Microsoft have introduced a bandwidth limit to windows update, which means you can allocate a percentage of your bandwidth to windows update so it doesn't use your entire bandwidth to download updates

The settings for this are buried inside windows update and you can find them here..

Settings app > update & security > windows update > advanced options > delivery optimization > advanced options.

You can also find the settings using Cortana Search. Just type in...

```
delivery optimization
```

Click on the best match at the top of the popup box.

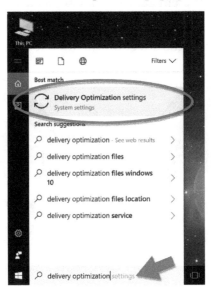

Here you can change the settings by dragging the sliders and selecting the check boxes to enable/disable limiting.

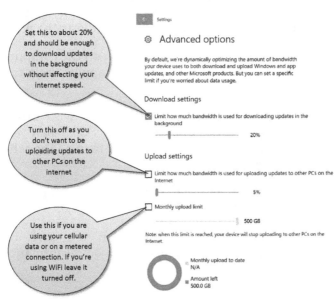

Disk De-fragmentation

Data is saved in blocks on the surface of the disk called clusters. When a computer saves your file, it writes the data to the next empty cluster on the disk, even if the clusters are not adjacent.

This allows faster performance, and usually, the disk is spinning fast enough that this has little effect on the time it takes to open the file.

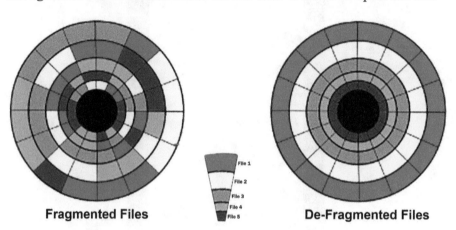

Fragmented Files   **De-Fragmented Files**

However, as more and more files are created, saved, deleted or changed, the data becomes fragmented across the surface of a disk, and it takes longer to access. This can cause problems when launching software (because it will often load many different files as it launches).

So bad fragmentation just makes every operation on the computer take longer but eventually fragmentation can cause applications to crash, hang, or even corrupt the data.

Disk defragmentation only applies to hard drives with mechanical spinning disks. If you have a solid state drive or SSD, then you don't need to worry about defragmentation and should turn off the scheduled optimisation on the drive.

It's a good rule of thumb to do this roughly once a month, to keep things running smoothly.

If you're using a solid state drive (SSD) then you don't need to defragment your drive, as it will have little effect on performance.

To de-fragment the disk in Windows 10, activate the search and type 'defragment'. Click 'Defragment and optimise your drives'.

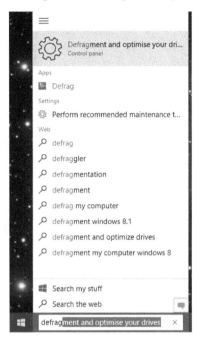

Select the drive your system is installed on, this is usually C. Click the 'optimize' button.

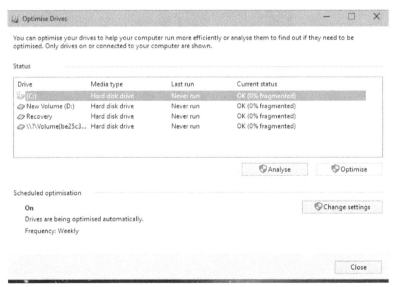

This will start de-fragmenting your disk. This process can take a while.

Disk Clean-Up

Over time, windows gets clogged up with temporary files from browsing the internet, installing and un-installing software and general every day usage. Doing this once a month will help keep things running smoothly.

Using the search on the taskbar, type 'cleanup'.

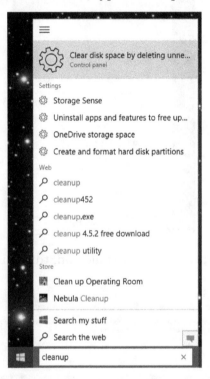

Click 'clear disk space by deleting unnecessary files'

Select drive C, click ok.

In the window that appears you can see a list of all the different files and caches. It is safe to select all these for clearing.

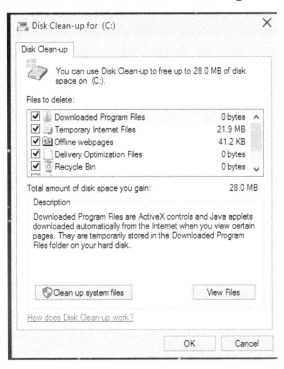

Once you are done click ok and windows will clear out all those old files.

Click 'delete files' on the confirmation dialog box to clear out all the old files

Do the same with the system files. In the window above, click 'clean up system files'.

This helps to keep your system running smoothly.

A good rule of thumb is to do this about once a month.

Start-Up Programs

Hit control-alt-delete on your keyboard and select task manager from the menu. Click more details if you don't have the screen below.

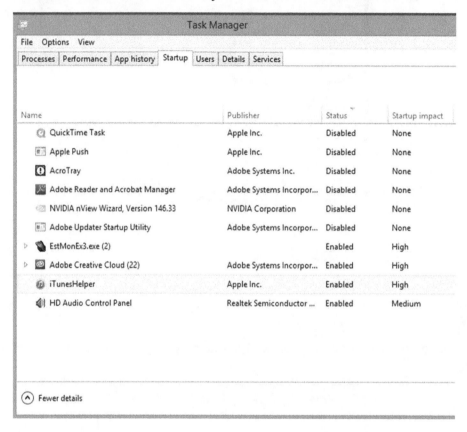

Click on the startup tab. Most of these programs can be disabled with the exception of your sound, video and network devices.

You will also see the startup impact this shows how much the program slows the machine down. These are the programs that show up in your system tray on the bottom right hand side of your screen. As you can see above, this system is quite clean – only essential icons appear in the tray.

If you are using a touch device you can access Task Manager by tapping the Search option on the start screen and type Task Manager. Then tap Task Manager in the list that appears.

Remove Programs and Apps

There are two ways you can remove programs, through the control panel or directly from the start menu.

For desktop apps such as anti-virus software, Microsoft Office, Adobe Creative Suite and similar apps, you should remove these from the 'programs and features' section of the Control Panel.

As an example, I am going to remove 'avast antivirus' from my computer.

First you need to open the 'programs and features' section of the control panel. The quickest way to do this, is to search for it using the search field on the bottom left of your task bar.

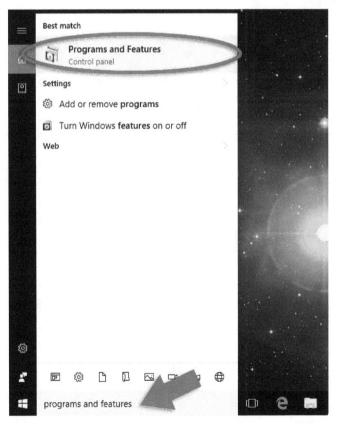

In the search field, indicated by the red arrow, type

```
programs and features
```

Click 'programs and features', circled above, from the search result.

Select the application you want to remove from the list, then click 'uninstall', circled below.

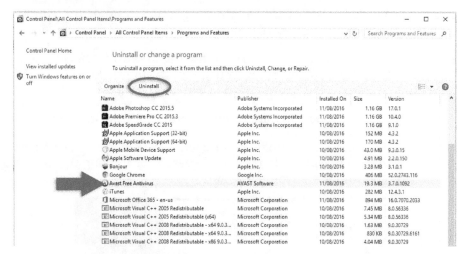

Now, depending on what program you are trying to remove, you might get a screen asking you what you want to do. In this case, avast is giving me options of what I can do.

In most cases you just have to click the 'uninstall' button, also sometimes labelled 'remove'.

Once you have done that, the install wizard will run and start to remove the software you have chosen. Depending on what you have chosen to remove, you might need to restart your PC.

This is a similar process for removing old versions of Microsoft Office or Adobe Creative Suite and any other desktop applications.

It's good practice to go through the apps and programs installed on your device, and remove the ones you don't use anymore and any old apps. This helps to keep your device running smoothly.

For apps that you have downloaded from the App Store and ones that come with Windows 10, you can remove them directly from the start menu.

Do this by right clicking on the icon on the start menu and selecting 'uninstall'. Tap and hold your finger on the icon, if you are using a touch screen tablet.

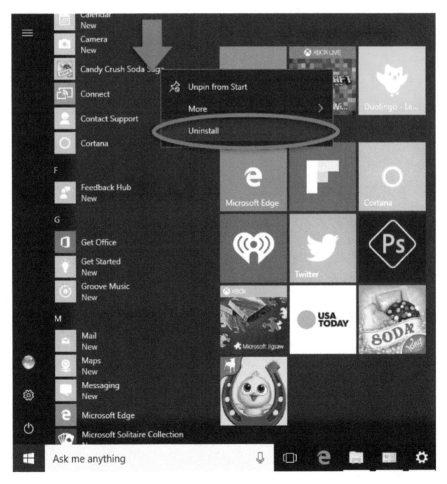

Resetting Apps

Sometimes apps can become slow and unresponsive, so in Windows 10, you have the option to reset the app. This will clear all the App's data, history lists, caches, settings and so on. This doesn't clear any of your personal files etc.

Settings App -> Apps -> Apps & Features.

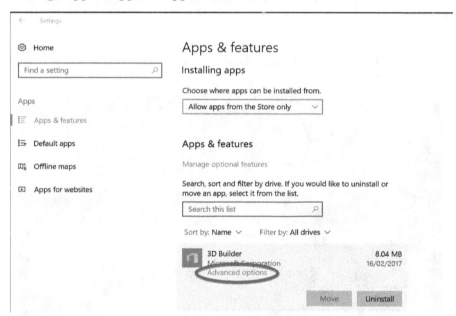

Tap on an App in the list, then tap 'advanced options'.

From the advanced options, tap 'reset'. Then tap 'reset' again to confirm.

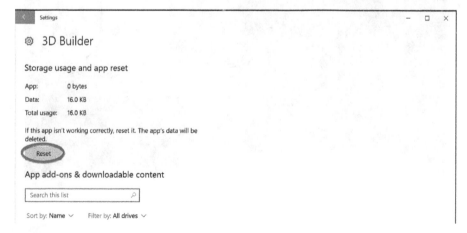

System Recovery

If you are having problems then Windows 10 has a section to recover your computer.

Go to settings on your start menu.

Click update & security

Click 'restart now'

When your machine restarts, it will boot into recovery mode.

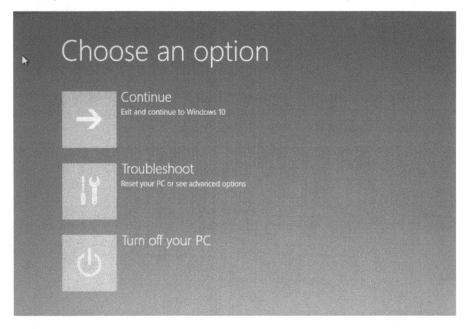

Clicking continue, will abort and return to windows 10.

Click 'troubleshoot' to enter recovery mode.

When in recovery mode you can click reset your PC.

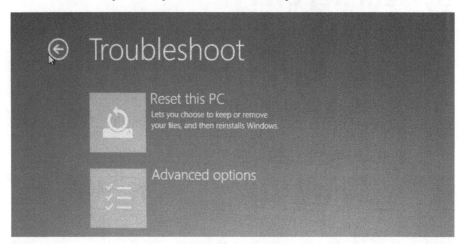

From here you can do a complete re-install by clicking on 'remove everything'. This will remove all your files and applications and reset Windows 10 back to its factory default.

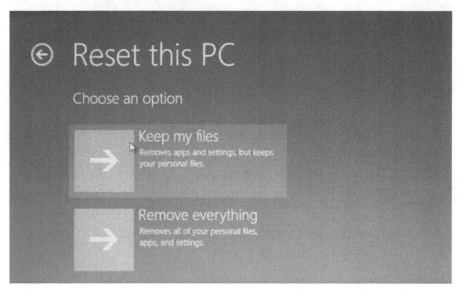

Clicking on 'keep my files', will refresh Windows 10, delete all your installed applications and settings. Your personal files and data will remain intact.

Advanced Start up

If you select 'Advanced Options' from the troubleshoot screen, there are a couple of useful features are 'system restore' which restores your PC to a previous state, for example if you installed a driver and its causing problems in windows.

Also 'System image recovery' if you created a recovery image disk. This can be used to restore windows from the image recovery disk.

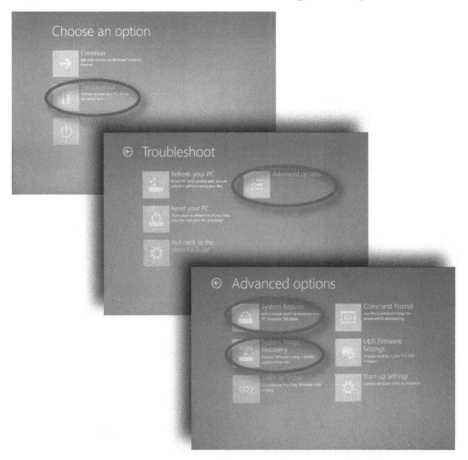

Insert your recovery disk and click 'system image recovery' to restore from a disk.

For information on creating images, see the next section.

Create a Recovery Drive

A recovery drive or recovery disk is an exact copy of your entire system often referred to as a 'system image'. This image contains your operating system (windows 10), settings/preferences as well as any applications.

This is useful if your computer crashes and you can't start it up again.

From Cortana's Search type 'backup and restore'.

Plug in a portable hard drive (a 500GB capacity is usually more than enough).

Click 'Create a system image', then select "on a hard disk".

Click next. Make sure only 'system reserved', 'system' & 'windows recovery environment' is selected. Click next.

You will be able to start windows with this drive if your computer fails. Use the procedure outlined in 'advanced start up' in previous section.

Some Useful Utilities

Here are a couple of useful utilities I have used over the years to keep my computers running smoothly.

Piriform CCleaner

CCleaner is a utility that allows you to clear out all the rubbish such as temporary files, programs that start automatically when you log in, web caches, log files, and settings that slow your computer down.

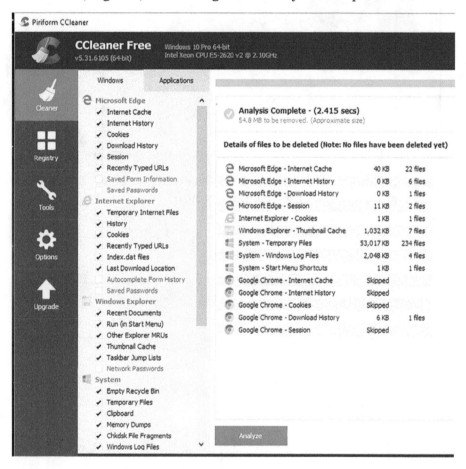

You can download the utility here...

www.piriform.com/ccleaner/download

Make sure you download this utility from this website ONLY and no other, as there are malware versions of this utility going around.

Malwarebytes

This utility detects and prevents contact with fake websites and malicious links. It can also detect and remove malware and is useful if your computer has become infected with some kind of adware or malware.

You can download it here...

www.malwarebytes.com

Click 'free download', then click 'run' when prompted by your browser.

You should NOT download this tool from any other website.

Index

Index

Index

V

W

CPSIA information can be obtained
at www.ICGtesting.com
Printed in the USA
BVHW06s0857171018
530416BV00015B/1300/P